SET YOUR THOUGHS FREE

A Program to Stay Off the Streets, Out of Prison, and Take Control of Your Life

RAUL BAEZ

First Stillwater River Publications Edition

ISBN: 978-1-960505-43-9

Library of Congress Control Number: 2023910735

1 2 3 4 5 6 7 8 9 10
Written by Raul Baez.
Published by Stillwater River Publications, Pawtucket, RI, USA.

Names: Baez, Raul, author.
Title: Set your thoughts free : a program to stay off the streets, out of prison, and take control of your life / Raul Baez.
Description: First Stillwater River Publications edition. | Pawtucket, RI, USA : Stillwater River Publications, [2023]
Identifiers: ISBN: 978-1-960505-43-9 (paperback) | LCCN: 2023910735
Subjects: LCSH: Baez, Raul. | Ex-convicts--United States--Biography. | Criminals--Rehabilitation. | Crime prevention. | LCGFT: Autobiographies. | Self-help publications.
Classification: LCC: HV9468.B23 A3 2023 | DDC: 364.8092--dc23

DEDICATION FOR YOU!

Do not conform to the pattern of this world but be transformed by the renewing of your mind. Then you will be able to test and approve what God's will is—his good, pleasing, and perfect will.

Romans 12:2

My brother, my sister, I want to introduce you to the principles I used to transform my toxic thinking into a world of possibilities. These principles are a compass on the road that yields successful outcomes. I promise you, this program will work—*if* you work. This means stepping into your inner self and accessing the untapped potential you have voluntarily neglected. You have the power to consciously make the choice to eradicate negative thinking into positive thinking. Let go of the belief that life is a constant struggle and create a life of prosperity, creativity, and joy.

If you have struggled with addiction or have been incarcerated, chances are we share some common denominators that have led us to these pervasive outcomes. Here's a sample of some struggles I had to abdicate to become the person I am today. I believe, based on the hundreds of workshops I've conducted, you will identify with what I'm going to share in some way.

A sense of adventure: I was always willing to roll up my sleeves and try something new, from food to employment. Others might see the unknown as scary; for me, it was life. While this may sound positive,

I was addicted to adrenaline, and it left me in a deficit. I could not focus on anything of substance, even if my life depended on it.

Adaptability: I could interact with all kinds of people in all kinds of places. I could change into character and I enjoyed playing these roles, even at the risk of having the outcome hurt me in some way. I was so adept at being someone else that I often lost myself along the way. I had no idea who I was, what I wanted out of life, who was important to me, or what was important to me. I was a master of many personalities and a fraud to myself.

Many interests: There was nothing that lacked my interest. I wanted to participate in anything within my limits. I could make stimulating conversation about almost any topic. If I didn't already know something, I was eager to learn to give the appearance I was intelligent and well-rounded. This was the primary influence that subjected me to external factors and other people driving my life.

Plan averse: Because I always believed in the idea that things will change, I had an unwillingness to plan in my future or relationships. This limited the possibilities of new and greater experiences. That put me in a position to let others tell me who I was and who I can become. That's great when you have the right people on your side, but in the presence of dysfunctional individuals, you become a monster. Monsters are either put in cages or killed. I was killed—emotionally, mentally, and psychologically. I lost hope for genuine outcomes that fill the heart. It led to multiple bouts of depression and suicide attempts.

Learned helplessness: Like so many others, it's easy to fall into the trap of thinking I have no control over a situation. I would often just give up and go on to the next thing. If you hear people say, "you can't" enough times, you start to internalize: "I can't." Eventually, it becomes true. That was my default way of thinking without ever considering that there must be a better way. You become what you think about, most of the time. Most of the time, I didn't believe it was in me to succeed. I gave value to everyone's opinion, affirming it without ever challenging it.

Unfocused: This is the dark side of uncertainty. You can get involved with too many things at once and become careless about yourself and others. People always told me I was unreliable, irresponsible, and a danger to all in my circle, including myself. Little did I know or understand that it was anger deriving from the mental, sexual, and physical abuse I endured in my formative years. It was fueling my foundation of toxicity in every area of life.

Addictive or destructive behaviors: Because I valued variety, my need for ever-changing stimulation ironically led to me developing patterns that make me feel certain I would get that variety. This manifested in various forms but had its most impact on my addiction and relationships. In other words, it gave me certainty that I would experience uncertainty. I was so submerged into this way of thinking that I did everything possible to stay in uncertainty. I was operating my life cuffed by this comfort zone only. I always had the power to do something but for 30-plus years I did not want to rock the boat if it meant I had to leave my comfort zone.

Finally, there came a time when I learned the virtues, values, and behaviors that go into becoming the person I aspire to be. When you become a well-disciplined person of high integrity, you will tend to live your life consistent with the essential virtues that make up the character of a superior person. You will inevitably embark on a life of freedom in every area of your life. Be open to new ideas and Set Your Thoughts Free!

This book is a roadmap created from personal experiences, education, trainings, books, and workshops I have held with hundreds of men and women. In the process, I've met many people who have never experienced addiction or imprisonment physically. However, they experienced the same emotions, fears, and doubt common with drug addiction and incarcerated experiences.

Their lenses with these emotions speak from a mental, emotional, and psychological self-incarceration with no release date in sight. Many have broken the cycles and are currently living life to the fullest.

My brother, my sister, you too can join us by using the tools in this book as a template to guide your journey of life after incarceration and/or addiction. I promise you, it will work if you work—so get ready to work! You cannot do something new with old-school thinking. The lessons you will ascertain will become ideals to abolish whatever is holding you back. Begin cultivating these principles and refine the outcomes in your life.

It is my prayer that you will be set free from the bondages robbing you of total access to unleashing your fullest potential!

CONTENTS

ACKNOWLEDGMENTS

A deep gratitude to my beautiful children—Brenda, Yelitza, Isaiah, and Jordan—and all eleven of my precious grandchildren. They gave me an honest and open opportunity to illustrate that I was not the man people said I was. We have developed a relationship, and all my greatest moments since my release starts with them. My life is nothing without you guys. Thank you for the incredible love, joy, and wonderful memories, both as adults and during your precious childhoods. My greatest moment is when we all sat together as a family, taking up a whole row in Harvest Field Community Church—Praise God!

Unfortunately, my youngest son and I are not in contact with each other, as of September 2019. I had him come live with me to guide him into his potential, but he espoused a diverged ideology. He will have to get there on his own and at his own time. My responsibility is to equip him to overcome his weaknesses and to step into adulthood.

The repudiation is his choice and therefore the task of reconciliation is his, too. The lesson: when opportunities knock, and your life is in disorder you must become humble and submit. Only you can procure it, nobody is ever going to give you that. Little does he know, there is not a second chance. He is on his own. I will stay in my lane, driving my priorities to guarantee peace and joy in my life, with or without him.

To my mother, thank you for birthing me and planting the seeds that have allowed me to become who I am. She could only do what she could with what she had at the time. I have forgiven my mother for all I did not get when I was supposed to get it. There are plenty of residual collateral consequences to my early childhood experiences. For me to live, I had to free myself from that past.

In my darkest moment, she became my biggest advocate, and therefore, I can move pass her shortcomings. She is loaded with toxicity, but I have made the choice not to allow her words or scope of how things should be to impair *my* choice to be who I choose to be. At sixty-one years old, I am still looking for my mother's love. I still lift her up, I still honor her as my mother. Today, as she struggles with memory loss through a chronic illness to her brain, I understand the best in her was already given to me. Though it wasn't good enough for me, I accept the fact I will never get the love I yearn from her. I remember, when I was facing all that time, how she would tell me God will make a way for me. The rest is history in the making.

To my sisters—Nancy, Neca, and Letty—for their unconditional love, support, and prayers. We have endured so much together growing up, but—thanks be to God—we have overcome them to live a meaningful life in abundance. I am proud of each one of you for the women you have become, despite all the madness we went through when growing up as teenagers in the Bronx. To my brother, Ruben, who—when he was alive—was the only man I had a meaningful relationship with. He knew all my secrets and all my pain. I have never trusted in anyone like I did my brother. I missed him like crazy. RIP, Ruby Dollars!

Lastly, to my sisters on the Baez side of the family: Ivette, Vanessa, China, and Lourdes. I lost contact with them around 1979/1980 and did not see them again until 2011. Despite losing all those years, upon learning the insanity I was living, they showed me that they never wavered from loving me.

I love getting together with them; we eat, we laugh, and we love one another because that is the only way to live and do family. Whenever I am invited, they all come out. My heart melts when I reflect on the memories we have developed since being reunited. I thank you with all my heart for allowing me to experience the love available through these family moments.

To the lady who tried to get me into a Christian drug program in the middle of the night and in the middle of purchasing drugs—I never went with you, but you never left me. I always think of the impact that encounter had in my life. God has revealed himself to me, despite the circumstances. I was once too broken to understand, hear, or see. Nonetheless, your obedience was fruitful. The seeds inevitably produced a phenomenal garden within me. This was the day prior to my last incarcerated experience.

To Javier Miranda, a fellow inmate at Eastern Correctional Facility. In 2002, Jay (as he was called) pinned me to the wall in the yard and confronted me with the fraud I was perpetuating to be.

He illuminated for me that as long I continued to feed my ego and addiction instead of my mind, I would never stay out of jail and therefore never become the father I claimed to be.

To Juan Padua, AKA Ponce, for inviting me to go inside the Protestant service at Eastern Correctional Facility so we could get some coffee and donuts and get out of the cold. I heard Mathews 11:28-30, and the words pierced my heart. The floodgates opened as I went to the altar and accepted Christ as my Lord and Savior. It was the first time I cried since the age of six.

To Eric Holmes, for introducing me to entrepreneurship and allowing me to connect how I can use it to create the job of my desire. That really got me to focus on eradicating my addiction and self-analyzing. Sometimes in life, there will be casualties so others can live. He saved my life as I choose to get the lessons from his failure to guarantee my success. I dug deep to find some answer in fear it would happen to me. Thank you, my brother!

To my inner spirit, whom I called God, for the silent whispers when I arrived at Otisville Correctional Facility in 2006 to start an entrepreneurial program. I had no idea what to do or how to get started, but the spirit of God took control, and the program became a pivotal endeavor in the transformation of my life.

To Andre Ward, AKA Imani, who stood up and offered the Nation of Islam room to conduct the entrepreneur classes. Amazingly, my biggest obstacle to implement the program were inmates, not administration. I was tapping into their donuts, movies, and other frivolous activities considered fun and popular. It was a pivotal and valuable lesson for me. In the pursuit of what we want, we must be committed to the cost of seeing it through. There will always be circumstances, people, and challenges enrooted, aiming to deviate our pursuit of achievements. The moment of adversity is to reaffirm the fire in your heart that first propelled you to move into the vision. Every time you stepped into it, you got closer—and then one day, it finally happened.

To Ray Rios, Mark Graham, and Johnny Lopez for introducing me to the concept of returning into the prison system as a volunteer after incarceration. They all return through a program called Residents Encountering Christ and introduced me to all kind of possibilities. Ray Rios and Johnny Lopez, respectively, were instrumental in my release, assisting me with my first job and getting me placed into an esoteric transitional house.

To Kenny Turner, my instructor at an MBA-style business program, for teaching me how to take a business and turn it into a company. More importantly, I was down on my dream of teaching financial literacy, and his words were desperately needed.

The essence of his aspiring words was that the types of businesses I wanted to switch to were already in abundance throughout a typical urban community. There were few, however, to teach financial literacy. He redirected me to my passion. He inspired me to pursue it because it was attainable.

To Marten Hoekstra, my mentor and a man I genuinely want to emulate. He is highly successful and respected in Wall Street and the world of Finance. Soon after the conversation with Kenny

Turner, I went to meet with Marten. He ignited a fire in me and my low self-esteem at the time. His passive yet piercing assessment of my potential to become an awesome entrepreneur propelled me to reevaluate my talents and gifts.

He told me anyone can sell chicken, but there are not many people that could serve my target market with both the personal and business acumen I had. I remember leaving his office that day to hug everybody I saw in the street. I reconnected with that inner spirit I call God and my life took on a new purpose to see this through. It made an enormous difference in my approach and mission. I went on to place in the finals in the business competitions following his advice and it was the turning point in my proclamation that failure is not an option and that only the attainment of my dreams will do. God used Marten and Kenny to restore my faith that what he started with me would be finished. Hallelujah!

Sonali and Austin finalized my renewed inspiration by contributing the business perspective I was lacking and needed. Particularly Sonali, who dedicated numerous hours from her hectic schedule to direct my focus and attention on the important matters. She took the time to give me honest and hard feedback about the things I needed to develop to be a true professional and what it takes to run a business. Her genuine compassion and authentic desire to see me succeed propelled me to dig deeper within myself. She would go as far as laying it out, so I had a guide to go by.

These were remarkably successful people on Wall Street, running million-dollar companies—and here they were, sharing their expertise, time, and love. That type of giving from the heart with the only purpose being to affirm my success—it floored me!

Finally, to all those I did not mention by name but who contributed to the sculpturing of my dreams and passion. It is not possible to name everyone. Rest assures, at its appropriate time, your significant contributions always get mentioned!

INTRODUCTION

I was born and raised in the Bronx, home of the 27-time World Champions—the New York Yankees. I was privileged to greatness. The problem was, I never ever imagined I could live out of greatness. I was always able to identify it in others, but never within.

I grew up in a household of sexual, physical, and emotional abuse. Everything I heard, everything I saw, was dysfunctional. Nobody ever empowered us to dream big. I never heard that the world is full of possibilities, or that you can become whatever you want. I never heard the words "I love you." I never celebrated a birthday; no one ever said, "you're cute," even though, as I now know, I was! At the age of six, I was sexually molested for the first time. I would experience numerous confrontations of abuse till the age of nine by three individuals.

I remember feeling so confused and scared, wondering why this didn't stop. I was terrified whenever one of them would be in the house that I would urinate in my pants and then get a whipping from my mom because I didn't go the bathroom. Finally, one day she asked me why, all of a sudden, I had a problem controlling my urine. I told my mother; she did not believe me. She slapped me so hard I fell to the floor. She grabbed me by the hair, yelling all kinds of threats, and then kicked me in the stomach with her knee. She made me promised never to talk about this again, so I didn't. The reality is, I was talking loudly, in destructive ways—but nobody was listening, and nobody ever heard me. These are the best recollections I have, as it relates to my emotions and thoughts as a child about these horrible experiences. I literally shut down, being obedient to my mom's demands that I never speak on this again. That directive ultimately removed it from my memory and thoughts. It wasn't until I started to confront these incidents that I was able to start peeling away the layers. I started to become transparent to myself and others, initiating my healing process.

I have a very limited amount of childhood memories beyond those I mentioned. As an adult, it became adamantly clear that I was consumed with shame, anger, isolation, an inability to trust, and a lack of respect for authority or rules. There are still situations or people that trigger that pain which is found in the anger and the shame. Today, as a Christian, I can rest in God's word for guidance with these difficult moments.

The three individuals who sexually molested me are dead now. I don't have the luxury of confronting them, which doesn't resonate well with me. My mom is losing her memory, either from dementia or Alzheimer's disease. That leaves me in a deficit to fill in the blanks and the why's. Today, I accept that this is what is, and I choose to focus on the things and people that bring me joy, peace, and love.

At the age of thirteen, I dropped out of school and embarked on a journey of hard-core drugs. When I stopped doing drugs, I looked up and realized I was thirty-nine years old. Those twenty-six years of insanity destroyed everything in my path, including my family. Addiction of any kind, but especially drugs, will pump absurdity into your life. I was not exempt, and that principle was pervasive throughout my addiction. It cost me jobs and opportunities to advance, my freedom for a collective twenty-three years of incarceration, and relationships. It caused multiple near-death experiences—six, to be exact! I lived in the abyss of collateral consequences due to drugs.

I was only thirteen years old when I had my first overdose. It was accidental; I took multiple tabs of mescaline, not cognizant that time was required before the effect of the drug would trigger. This lack of understanding led to me taking a second tab to experience the effect I was anticipating. It exploded in my system. It was a hot summer day when I climbed the fence to a condominium complex so I could access the pool. I dove from a diving board into an empty pool, breaking three vertebrae and sustaining a massive scar on my forehead. The blood gushing on my face intensified my body temperature, making me feel like I was baking in an oven. It propelled me to find some cooling relief, so I took off all my clothes. I was ball-ass naked and screaming when I was confronted by the police. I was subdued and taken in an ambulance to the hospital. Then hospital staff inserted tubes into my stomach. I was resistant, withdrawing the tubes multiple times. I was inevitably restrained, which is the last thing I can remember from that day. I am not sure if I passed out or they induced me with medication.

When I awoke, I was in a single room in Bronx Psychiatric Center and my eyes were pinned on this beautiful young black woman. I was astonished as she mimicked the sound of a crying baby and then yelled at this imaginary baby to shut up. The depiction was enacted numerous times—then, she suddenly withdrew one of her breasts to feed the illusory baby. I started making the crying baby sound and, within a few seconds, she came over and put it in my mouth. I took her into the bathroom for privacy and had her perform oral sex. I experienced sexual pleasure for the first time in my life. This was my choice; I was not forced. Today, I realize my actions were manipulative. I rendered to this woman the learned behavior from all my sexual abuse encounters.

At the age of fourteen, I became a father to a premature baby. It was February, 1976. She was born weighing two pounds, four ounces, very fragile. She developed a serious infection in her intestine, as the formula she was receiving was too strong, and she required immediate surgery. She died at the age of twenty-two days. The technology in the seventies was not what it is today, for these babies.

Approximately two or three months later, I experienced a second overdose. This time I was attempting to commit suicide. I took a pill bottle containing valiums. I do not recollect how many I took, but it was about eight pills. I was lacking control. The last thing I remember was chasing my mother with an enormous kitchen knife. The police were eventually called. I climbed a fire escape to my grandmother's apartment where I had been living. My memory is totally blank thereafter. I was again admitted to a psychiatric ward. I was discharged upon completing a twenty-one-day evaluation and attending a court hearing for the assault charges against my mom. I was ordered into the custody of Division For Youth (DFY). I was acquitted after spending two or three weeks at Spofford Juvenile Center. Then, I went back to my granny's house.

In September 1976, my grandmother called the cops and turned me and my brother in, as she could not deal with our insanity no more. I was so infuriated; she snitched on me and my brother. As juveniles, we were sentenced to eighteen months for forty-eight counts of armed robberies, possession of heroin, and possession of a 38 Barretta with two 410 pump shotguns/six shot. I had just turned fifteen and my brother was fourteen…how crazy is that, huh?

In 1991, my girlfriend, Gisela, was pregnant with my youngest son, Jordan. She was about seven or eight months along at the time. I started playing with a 9mm Glock. I deliberately put the gun on Gisela's head. She was frantic, screaming and begging me to stop playing with the gun. For some strange reason, I was freaking enjoying it. To this day, I cannot define the reason. The more she screamed, the more I enjoyed it. I took the gun and placed it on her belly.

She really went berserk! I was really, really freaking enjoying this. I took the gun and put it in my mouth after telling her about the pain for her to live with would be greater if she could see me killing myself. In my mind, I was so sure the gun was empty since I knew the cartridge was removed. The problem was, I had left a bullet in the chamber and completely forgot about it.

I kept alternating the position of the gun to her head, her belly and back to my mouth numerous times, just enjoying the moment, as if I were celebrating. When Gisela finally reached a level of insane proportion with her screams, I yelled that the gun was empty and pulled the trigger—narrowly beating death a third time in my life. I was frozen, paralyzed in my thoughts, and started crying for about ten minutes. I really thought this gun was empty.

I was going to pull the trigger while the gun was in my mouth. At the very last minute, I decided to aim at the wall instead and when that shot came out, I could not believe how I just escaped death. Though I always kept a gun, after that encounter, I never played with it again. You would think, after an experience like that, that I would never buy another gun. I did not get the lesson and, in not doing so, continued to repeat the cycle and the madness in my life with guns.

In January 1992, my brother and best friend Ruben died from AIDS complications. The fact was he would not stop doing drugs, and that consumed his compromised immune system. He had survived a fifth-floor drop out of his bathroom window from a possible overdose three years earlier. He completely shattered his hip and, after that, could only walk with a severe limp from the imbalance. The injuries were insufficient to keep him from going to prison after being discharged from the hospital. Though the judge was lenient, he mandated him for two years. He was out of prison for less than a year before he died. The last five years of my brother's life really devastated me. I had some serious mental health issues evolving, unbeknownst to me at the time.

At the age of seventeen, I was finally a full-fledged dad. I walked into that responsibility with the luggage of trauma I had accumulated over the years, and without any counseling. I never got the answers to my drama. I never got fixed. I could not give my son something I did not possess. I never got loved, therefore, I could not give love to him, either. My son inhibited all the anger, rage, and bitterness I had mastered to camouflage my pain. In 1993, at the age of seventeen, he went to the streets with that chip on his shoulder, selling drugs in the Bronx. He was shot and killed. Growing up, I always heard it said that men are naturally wired to provide and protect. Losing my son made me feel inadequate, powerless. I could not protect him. I saw all the signs and unequivocally knew he was selling drugs and endangering himself. He was a calf amid wolves. I regret never having a conversation that could have possibly altered the direction of his life. The guilt consumed me. It manifested five years later when my oldest daughter, Brenda, was trapped in a domestic violence situation.

I had taught her to do whatever it takes to stand up to anybody abusing her, and she did! She stabbed her boyfriend—and was arrested for the assault. I was devasted and that guilt was amped up one thousand degrees. I felt so guilty and responsible for asking my daughter to resort to violence. My delusional reality led me to believe I had to rescue her, as if I were a freaking lifeguard.

I set up a drug dealer I used to buy drugs from to rob him. I needed money; I was determined to hire an elite lawyer to get my daughter out of jail. I took out my gun and he lunged to take it from me. I shot him twice. I really believed he was dead. There was no movement, and I didn't see any breathing. I couldn't believe what just happened and how quickly this got out of control. I was so petrified of the situation I created.

I was shaking uncontrollably. I couldn't focus; my heartbeat was pounding. I looked at the blood on my hands, and in an instant started thinking, *My life is over.* I knew that murder in New York is twenty-five years to life. In that moment, looking to control what I couldn't control, I made the decision to go on the run. *I will never go to jail for this,* was my thinking. I left my victim there in a pool of blood because I really thought he was dead, and I thought if I stayed any longer, I would be going to prison for the rest of my life.

There I was, homeless, nowhere to sleep, shower, or eat, and no money. My answer to eradicate the barriers of survival was to commit robberies. I did it every day or every other day for seven months.

Seven months equates to 210 days. The number of years I was facing if I just got the minimum for each robbery was over 200 years.

I made the decision that going to prison was not an option, so when the day came that I finally got arrested, I was determined to die rather than face incarceration. All my emotions at this point of my life spoke of the hopelessness and pain I was enduring throughout my life. I felt completely worthless; I could not imagine overcoming the barriers I faced ahead of me.

During the last robbery I committed, I deliberately shot at two NYPD officers to provoke suicide by cop. We do know, if you point a gun at an officer, they are going to shoot—and rightfully so! They shot thirty-two times, and—Glory to God—not one bullet hit me. Hallelujah! It was an unreal scene; the smell of gunpowder was thick in the air. There was damage everywhere—cars, windows from multiple dwellings. There was a stillness afterward, a quietness you cannot even imagine.

I locked eyes with the two officers and could easily detect the fear in them. They were both in their twenties, which saved me from getting shot. If they had been veteran police officers, they would have made Swiss cheese out of me. I started to flee from the scene and turned around to notice they were not coming after me. I cut through an alley and instantly concluded: *I am not running anymore. This is going to end today.* I could not bear the pain anymore.

I was inevitably pinned up in an alley with no hostages, surrounded by a SWAT team for four to five hours. I was starting to withdraw from the drugs and became extremely anxious. It was February 28, 1998, and it was extremely cold out. It is my belief that the combination of both the cold and the anxiety led me to apply pressure to the trigger as I held the gun to the side of my head. A shot went off toward the SWAT team. I was contemplating how this was going to end. I was not trying to shoot myself at all—I was waiting for the SWAT team to do it. Yes, I was a coward for sure! The SWAT team never shot, never! I shot at two of their officers and not one shot went off from them. I have multiple red beam lights from their weapons all over my body, and they did not shoot. They could have emptied out their arsenals, but they did not. There were no witnesses, yet they did not shoot.

There was no way I was supposed to survive both the shoot out and what transpired in this alley. Praise God, I did survive! When that shot went off, I defecated in my pants. I had no control, it just happened. I was really confused, scared, and could not comprehend what was happening. All I heard was screams by the SWAT team to put the gun down. My left eardrum was hurting immensely. I ruptured my eardrum from the shot going off. I was bleeding with profound pain.

In that brutal moment, a peaceful voice appeared to me with the words: *put the gun down.* In the moment of complete disorientation, mental and emotional, that voice was so comforting. It felt safe. I put the gun down.

Today, I understand God had his hand on me. I wasn't supposed to die that day because there was a greater purpose in my life. I just didn't know it at the time, I didn't see it, and I certainly wasn't feeling it. The voice instructing me to put the gun down was divinity.

During the judicial process of my arrest, I learned the individual I shot, the drug dealer, never died. He survived. The only thing that tied me to the crime was that I still had the same gun. He never surrendered my name as the shooter. I was stunned this man was still alive. I realized that all this time running, living in the streets for seven months, and all the ensuing acts of crime I perpetrated, were part of my purpose. The only way and the only place I would be able to find God—and, in finding God, finding my purpose—was by going to prison.

Being homeless forced me to believe the only way to overcome it was to commit robberies. It was the only way I knew to find the money I needed to survive being homeless. I needed funds for eating, staying in motels, and feeding my addiction. I committed a robbery every day or every other day for seven months. Seven months, remember, equates to 210 days, so at the very least I probably committed 100 to 150 robberies. It was all I knew how to do to generate money, yet the outcome clearly speaks. I wasn't very proficient at it.

I was running from a crime that was not even tagged to me or my name. Later in my transformational process, I came to realize that even difficult moments in life have a purpose to shape who we become. I needed to go through the fire to get what I needed for breaking the shackles holding me back in life.

When you shoot at a police officer, they try to get every charge against you to raise the number of years they can put you away. Again, rightfully so! These men and women have a difficult and dangerous job. They have as much right to go home to their families as anyone else. If we did not have them doing their jobs, can you imagine what NYC would look like? With no police officers? We need to respect these brothers and sisters—period! I tell you one thing: if you ever become a homeowner, you will appreciate them, and the work they perform, for preserving your home values.

This man I shot would not testify against me. There are only two realistic reasons why he wouldn't, and both derived from living and growing up in the streets. To the average person that doesn't come from that environment, they may view it as totally insane, but it is not:

1. He was contemplating street justice. Revenge. He wanted to kill me himself.
2. He was afraid of my family, whose reputation in the streets was to resolve any conflict with violence.

They could not charge me for shooting him, and so those charges went away. If the victim that got shot would not testify, there was no way a jury would find me guilty.

About three weeks later, while waiting for a court appearance on the charges pending from the day of my arrest at Rikers Island, I got picked up for a whole week's worth of line-ups. I cannot give an exact number. It was every day, all day that whole week. The fact is, there were enough line-ups to put me away for the rest of my life. All those robberies I committed were tied to me for the similarities of appearance, because I wore a suit to all my robberies. It completely blindsided my victims.

They didn't expect me to rob them, since I was wearing a suit. I had the same gun and gave the same instructions to intimidate and control everyone present. I would tell them I already killed one person so killing another would not be an issue for me. I had everyone's absolute attention and cooperation to the fullest. The outcome: not one person could ID me in those line-ups. Therefore, if I wasn't ID'd, I could not be charged for a single robbery. Let us be noticeably clear: God had his hand on all these events! I eventually accepted a plea bargain for fourteen years to abdicate the charges stemming from the day I got arrested. The initial charges were attempted murder on a police officer, which got reduced for my plea agreement to armed robbery in the first degree.

During my first six years of incarceration, nothing changed within me. I was still doing drugs. Yup, there are plenty of drugs in prison. In fact, it may be easier to buy drugs in an institution than it is to walk through a neighborhood in New York City. The drugs are a lot more expensive than on the streets, but they are readily available in every prison.

One year short of the halfway mark to my incarceration, I was circling the yard at Eastern Correctional Facility in Napanoch, NY with an acquaintance. We decided to enter the chapel for some shelter from the cold. The goal was to get some coffee and donuts, let the hands get warm for a few minutes, and then depart. When we entered, a visitor from Prison Fellowship Ministry was starting the service. The words pierced my heart, and the floodgates opened!

"Come to me, all you who are weary and burdened, and I will give you rest. Take my yoke upon you and learn from me, for I am gentle

*and humble in heart, and you will find rest for your souls. For my
yoke is easy and my burden is light."*

Mathews 11:28-30

Those words were so reassuring and comforting to me. I had
no idea of the true meaning of what I heard until years later when
I really got into Bible study. The power of God's word cannot be
defined as it moves into people's hearts in infinite ways and can't be
contained in one explanation. He is massive, powerful, able to reach
anyone, anywhere and at any time, HALLELUJAH!

I accepted God into my life that day but still, nothing changed on
the inside. I continued to seek God for the next two years, playing
games. I would go into the Bible studies and services stoned out of
my mind on heroin. I would be nodding and praising God. I was
smoking and smelling like an ashtray, cursing, and still focusing on
all the madness of my past.

One night, I finally got on my knees to pray for my daughter,
Yelitza, who was enduring a serious heart condition. She needed surgery to regulate her heartbeat. I was also overwhelmed with anxiety in anticipation of settling a drug debt. In prison, these debts
are resolved in violence. Though I did owe the money, I didn't want
to resolve it with violence anymore. I was finally seeing the streets
within reach and my main objective now was to be with my kids. I
didn't want to miss any more of their lives as I started to understand
the collateral consequences of being incarcerated for so many years. I
gradually started to see it was possible for me.

God's response to this prayer overwhelmed me with his grace.
My daughter was fully recovered. The individual I was preparing to
battle apologized for threatening me. This person was a wolf in the
system and well known in the state. In prison, the more violence you
perpetrate, the more you are respected. An apology in prison is a sign
of weakness.

This was my defining moment with God. I learned how to depend on God from these two experiences. When I did my prayer, I was attempting to manipulate God, con the creator of the universe. I was lying to God the way I was lying to everybody else, including myself! God answered that prayer in such a way that I was touched by his grace and completely surrendered. Praise God.

From that day forward, I stopped hanging out with the lunatics in prison. Yup, there's some crazy people in prison. I stopped listening to destructive music. I gave up watching TV. Within months my worldview of people, life, family, and God had shifted into something I never had experienced in my life. In the Bible, Proverbs 23:7 reads; "As a man thinketh in his heart, so is he." That Bible truth became one of my foundational principles. It totally changed the way I saw things.

The outcomes were so massive and extreme that the emotional connection to these experiences propelled me to seek more. I had an appetite for meaningful results, defined as, success begets success.

My spiritual growth empowered me to implement the same principle in my relationships, finance, education, my family, my goals. This paradigm shift propelled me to achieve meaningful outcomes.

Here within, is the essence of this book. The book will illustrate, step by step, how to impart these concepts by easing your entry into this new way of living. You will renew the belief that you can accomplish whatever you desire.

The only thing, and the only person, preventing the attainment of your goals is *you!* You can transform your minimal thinking, your negative energy, your reliance on the opinions of other people, and your thoughts. You can develop new lenses through which you can live life from today. It is my hope that you will take these new concepts and incorporate them into your life. The book will speak to you, it will be a call of action. If you do heed this call, congratulations—you will experience meaningful outcomes. To the degree you embrace these concepts, you are guaranteed to go higher in your life, I promise!

My name is Raul Baez, and I approve this message!

1

THE VISION ~ WITO'S LEGACY

I am proud and humble to have your attention with my life's work. The genesis of my book is found in my son, Wito. I received an inspirational voice while incarcerated at Otisville Correctional Facility in 2006 to reach out to the young men I observed going home and coming back. I was perplexed with the reasons why so many could not stay jail-free and drug-free, instead voluntarily surrendering years of their lives to the insanity of prison. I stepped into that voice by working with one individual, which then turned into ten. These ten soon became the inspiration for creating a program to offer them character development, business ideation, and real estate principles. It was a progressive curriculum to develop the necessary thinking required before change is possible in the first level, the various entity structures with proving concepts of a legitimate business in the second level, and how to buy your first property in the third level.

Those familiar with prison programming understand it is antiquated and irrelevant to equip individuals as they transition back into society. I became motivated to use my experiences and resources to empower these young men. I felt an urgency to eradicate the dynamics subjugating their minds.

The program was a great success! That success is not only measured by what took place behind the wall, but upon being released as well.

It took me two years to get the program running. The administration kept rejecting my proposal. With each rejection I focused on how to overcome the "no." I would extinguish the barrier and they would pose a new one. This two-year journey sculpted within me the habit of perseverance and the habit of focusing on solutions. I discovered the gifts of being creative and persistent. This ignited in me the realization that if I was able to accomplish all this in prison, when I got home, I already knew the world was mine.

I required the assistance, knowledge, support, and time of so many to reach my goal. In prison, you cannot control anything and are reliant on others for almost anything you want or need. That dependency taught me patience, a crucial dynamic for success. Many incarcerated individuals also ascertain this skill, but when they get home, this skill is precipitously degenerated. There are many skills developed in prison that equip individuals for greater outcomes. Many however, are determined to exterminate them from their toolbox. They extinguish essential components that would maximize their potential to stay jail-free. They cherry-pick ownership of the ways of thinking and behaviors in prison.

Prison is an abnormal environment where people resort to abnormal thinking and behaviors. This permeating thinking and behaviors force people to equate conventional thinking and behaviors as abnormal. In other words, abnormal thinking and behaviors are accepted as being normal over time. This mindset is perpetrated in every instance, and forces a person to project the gladiator mentality necessary to thrive in prison. In prison, if you cross someone's path and do not ask to be excused or apologize, it is disrespectful, and you could be killed for the violation. If you change the TV without checking in with everyone present, you are deemed to be disrespecting the audience and could be killed. Every confrontation is engulfed in violence. The more violence you enact, the more you are respected. If you do not, you are labeled weak, and the men considered to be wolves will inevitably challenge you in some way. Every dispute in prison is resolved with violence. There's no, "Let's talk about what happened, how can we avoid conflict," etc. Apologies are a sign of weakness. The ultimate resolution is to extract blood. I am not hyping this up; this is the hardcore reality of imprisonment, especially in a maximum-security prison. Many men go home with this mentality. They bring it into work, becoming argumentative. They manifest it in their relationships, compromising the integrity of the relationship. It all leads to the feelings of failure and rejection. These negative feelings eventually lead to the same terrible thinking and behaviors that led to prison in the first place. Hence, the cycle is born and continued.

The program was called E.R.I.C., which stood for, Entrepreneur Real estate Investment Course. Immediately, it became the number one program at Otisville correctional facility. Before we inaugurated the first class, we already had a waiting list for the two ensuing classes. We only had capacity for twenty-five individuals at a time. Each cycle consisted of twenty-six weeks, meeting for one hour per week. It was designed with the purpose of challenging individuals to tap into their unique skill sets.

The goal was to stimulate their appetite for higher education. Here within, the foundation for developing academic skills were instituted. Remember, one of the influential factors motivating me to construct the program was for the purpose of equipping these young men with tangible skills for success. I submerged myself into the program and, in the process, found purpose. The success of the program helped me connect to my son in a way I never experienced when he was alive. I never had a meaningful conversation with my son that addressed the challenges in life. I never deposited inspirational thoughts or models that nourished growth. I never found words of empowerment. Everything I exposed him to how to survive in the streets—"don't tolerate anything from anybody," "make sure you walk away winning your street battles," "do whatever it takes, including the use of violence." I was really broken and wanted to instill in him the value of hurting others before they hurt you.

As I worked with these young men, they reminded me so much of my son. I learned to express my fears, my aspirations, my desire to see them win. I built strong and deep relationships with them. I was seen as a father figure, which I deeply appreciated. It gave me validity that I can be looked upon as a leader, as a father, as a mentor. We would cry together, we would tell each other how much we love each other, and the trust we developed was so strong. Many of us agreed, we never experience these things in our real families. In this process, I became highly motivated to do this work for the rest of my life. Purpose is doing something you love so much that you'd do it for free, but that you do it so well you get compensated well for doing it. This was the goal I set for myself.

When I was released from prison, I started a sole proprietorship entity to teach the same curriculum. That business led me to start an S-Corp after completing my MBA business program with Defy Ventures. Defy is an organization that teaches formerly incarcerated individuals an intense business program. The name is appropriate, as it aims to work alongside individuals to create a business, stimulating the probability of a successful transition and defying the odds. They have access to an elite group of professionals in the financial sector on every level including representation from senior management in Wall Street institutions.

Many are gurus in finance, and some are world-known celebrities.

The sole proprietorship had me charging one individual $50 for one hour. The S-Corp allowed me to get the same $50 for one hour also, but instead of teaching it to one individual, I started teaching it to fifty or 100 individuals an hour. I was introduced to this concept by my mentor, Marten Hoekstra. Marten was a Wall Street CEO for a major global bank. He taught me how to run a company, not a business. The success of those two reaffirmed my purpose and vision.

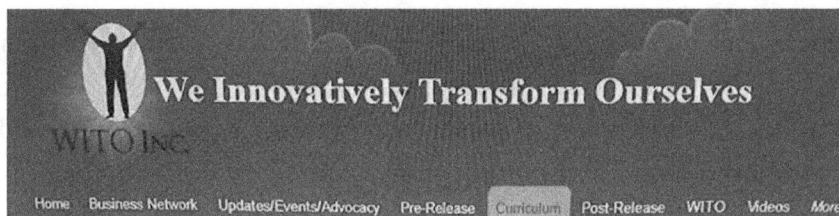

At the birth of that vision, it was clear to me that I wanted to dedicate my life to working with those left behind in prison. This motivated me to start a non-profit: WITO Inc. Wito, my son's nickname, was the inspirational force leading me to the vision. It was his story. I wanted to honor him and create a legacy so his name would live forever. WITO is an acronym which stands for, We Innovatively Transform Ourselves.

I chose a logo which defined what it felt like when I finally decided to take a stand. I envisioned myself on a rock, a solid foundation of principles worth living from. This is my place of surrender. I extended my hands upward, and the world was suddenly open to me, my dreams, and my aspirations.

Vision is foresight, is seeing the invisible and making it visible. It is an informed bridge from the present to a better future. Be empowered to create a picture and hold, in your mind's eye, the way things could or should be. If you can get there in your mind, you can get there in your reality. Vision connotes a visual reality, a portrait of a preferred future. The picture is internal and personal to you. There is nothing preventing you from cultivating a vision except the words, verbs, and adjectives of your destructive past. There is no bogeyman, except for those created by your own accord.

The way you practice is the way you will play the game of life. Champions become champions by dedicating themselves to repetition every day. No one has permission to present anything that is not aligned with the pursuit of being the absolute best. That is the drive of a true champion. If you want to be that champion, you must transform your thinking and motivation. Be an active participant in the arrangement of your future. Be methodical, be systematic in what you do, the order which you do it, and who you do it with. I invite you to start practicing wherever you are, with what you got—and start now!

I have been privileged to work with over 1200 men and woman transitioning from incarcerated experience. Along the way, I was able to ascertain data. That data is a definitive measure of the actual outcome. It is unambiguously and unequivocally true that those who practice what a successful transition will entail are more likely to succeed. The numbers do not lie: 87 percent of those with a realistic release plan who created the mental pictures prior to release were later pursuing their goals and living meaningful lives. Remember, the vision is personal to you. Do not emulate someone else's vision. Be free to take components of it, but do not dare to replicate. Those coming home need to be equipped with something tangible to succeed.

The reality is, you will be asked to start your life over upon release with $40 and perhaps a chiseled body. In New York, when you are released, you will depart with $40 to take a bus that, for most, lands them in Port Authority on 42nd street. If you have ever been there, you have seen thousands of people traveling in and out of the terminal. Imagine finding yourself in this fast-paced environment for the first time in ten, twenty, or even thirty years—what do you think it is going to feel like? The feedback I've gotten from the men and women in this situation is that they feel out of place—the joy of being released is decomposed. Some start to question and doubt whether they could move forward into free a society, feeling paralyzed, without even taking the first step into their freedom. They have already quit, mentally. I've even gotten some people say they were waiting for instructions before coming to their senses and deciding what's next. More commonly, they described anxiety, being apprehensive, lacking confidence, and feeling agitated and extremely worried.

The Department of Corrections has just released you there. You are now fully responsible to start your life all over again. Think about that, my brother and sister—what are the intricate parts you will need to augment your freedom forever? You will immediately encounter a technological world and a drastically different world. The more years you have been incarcerated, the more difficult it will be for you to navigate this new world. If you are going home with limited or no employable skills or education, you have a mountain to climb. You are simply not going to enter this world and turn a light switch on and have everything magically in place for you to thrive.

You must have a detailed plan. You must have focus. And even with that, you will be sailing in rough waters. It will not be as easy as you think. You must dedicate your time, thoughts, energy, and resources, into a path that will never take you back to prison.

How bad do you want it? Are you ready to pay the price in advance? If the answer is yes, welcome, my brother, my sister. Let's do this. I am inviting you to anchor yourself in the belief that things are possible for you. All you must do is open yourself up and declare that you can be innovative and transform yourself. I implore you to believe this and trust the process, trust the information, and trust the curriculum.

WITO Inc, was created to fulfill the mission of equipping incarcerated men and women with financial empowerment and transforming values so they can unlock the doors to success. It is my belief, the recidivism of those involved in a reentry plan will be reduced by outlining the possible barriers faced upon their return to the community and the solutions to abdicate them. It is my hope that you take advantage of the information in this book. The goal is to help you identify the many challenges you will face upon released, and then to strengthen your mental powers and skills to overcome those barriers. This book deals with the mental process to prepare you for success, however you define that term.

If you had to sell everything in your possession, how much would you get? That is your net worth! For many of the men and women coming home, that equates to the $40 gate fee upon release. I had to separate the books because, without changing your thinking, you will not change the behaviors and therefore the necessary outcomes we are striving for. I could give you $100,000, but if you do not change your mindset, you will blow the money in same fashion. Many athletes and movie stars do exactly that, after the career is over. They retired with the assumption life is one big party, but then have to come out of retirement when all that money disappears.

You can successfully transition from incarceration. I encourage you to study and take advantage of the material in these pages. Many have gone before you with a positive attitude and, after implementing the strategies conveyed within, went onto lead meaningful, productive lives. If you want to accomplish what others have, do the things they do and inevitably you will arrive at the same destination. Success leaves tracks, and the footprints are all laid out for you to replicate with equal or greater results.

The ultimate answer to this outcome of defining your success is determined by what you are willing to do and sacrifice to assure your arrival to that preset destination. You really do have the control; the pen is in your hands. Decide to write the ensuing chapters in your life where you get to illustrate to the world that you are an epic star. The choice is always yours, so take responsibility and step into your greatness.

The birth of my mission was to work with individuals in prison. While stepping into this calling in a free society, I came to work with individuals who have never been in a physical prison, but who were locked up in a mental, emotional, and psychological prison. I came to learn that they have inadvertently and voluntarily self-incarcerated. This shocking revelation also exhibited that their imprisonment is *worse* than a literal prison, and therefore more hellacious to extract oneself from. Most people in a physical prison have a release date, but the self-incarcerated do not—unless they really work for their escape. If you have self-incarcerated, the principles of this book will certainly liberate you from years, decades, or even generations of pain, shame, guilt, and fear.

You may be physically free, yet are experiencing an abyss of incarcerated emotions. The feelings of isolation, hopelessness, anger, and bitterness are pervasive, as is the belief and acceptance that your current situation is fixed forever. You feel and believe there's nothing you can do to get better and move forward. In fact, you defend the state you're in, proclaiming, "that's life." You may be enduring an enormous amount of suffering commonly induced by a noxious stimulus. You probably are waiting on someone to come to the rescue. Sadly, no one is coming. *You* are the calvary, *you* hold the key to liberation. I propose you take a stand embracing these principles as well. Just as I promised you, this program will work if *you* work. Dedicate yourself to freedom and breaking the cycles. I support your endeavors as you experience a life worth living. Best of luck to you! Go back with a renewed mind and sculpt your legacy!

There are two ways to get to the top of an oak tree. One: sit on an acorn and wait. Two: start climbing, See you at the top!

2

WHERE DO I BEGIN?

Let us begin by doing a fun exercise. Let's take a moment to release any fear, doubt, or mental barriers preventing you from receiving the ideology. Take a chance and follow these instructions. Trust what you are being asked to do and it will come together.

These exercises we are embarking on will illuminate insights on which negative thinking and behaviors you may be able to eradicate. It will express a purview on the way you respond in certain situations (especially when it comes to what I like to describe as the "jail mentality"). You will need some pen and paper before you can begin. Ideally, get a notebook to record the many strategies deriving from the book.

On this blank piece of paper, at the upper left-hand corner, please sign or print your name. Remember: trust the process, and do the exercise as I explain it.

Now draw a horizontal line across the whole page to separate the first task from task number two. Now underneath this line, sign or print your name again—this time, use your opposite hand. If you're right-handed, write it with your left hand, and vice versa. Take a moment to reflect what you're thinking and feeling when you receive these instructions, and then after you execute them. Be as concise and accurate as possible. This is for you; no one else will see it.

Now draw another line underneath. For task number three, write the word "MULTITASK" with your feet.

Just kidding, of course. Use your normal hand for writing. From this point forward, all the ensuing exercises will be conducted with your natural hand. Please write a summary of your thoughts and feelings as you execute the task. Please pay attention—soon, you may experience an exuberant amount of new revelations, which may alter the course of your life. Draw a line to perform the next task.

Please read the following instructions carefully before executing the next task. You will now write the word "multitask" but will do so in the following order: do the first letter, then the underline, and finish it out with the number in that exact order. It is imperative you do it in the exact order for optimization. Start with the letter M, and immediately underneath, place the number one. Then, do the same for each sequential letter with its corresponding number in the exact manner. Do not write out the word first and then enter the numbers, or you will sabotage the exercise.

M then do U then L then T then I then T then A then S then K
1   2   3   4   5   6   7   8   9

When you are done, chart number 1 should look just like this:

M U L T I T A S K
1 2 3 4 5 6 7 8 9

Begin the task of connecting with your emotions and thoughts.

Now please do the exact same exercise again, except you will include a letter of the alphabet after placing the number. You will start with the letter M and follow that up by placing the number 1 underneath—then, to complete the first column, you will place the alphabet letter A underneath the 1. Then you will go on to the next letter in multitask, *U*, followed by placing the number *2* and concluding with the alphabet letter *B*.

Continued the format till completion with the remaining letters in the word *multitask*, ending with the letter *K*, of course, above with the appropriate number (9) and the alphabet letter *I*. One letter at a time, one number at a time, and one alphabet at a time in that order. Chart number 2 should look like this at its completion:

M U L T I T A S K
1 2 3 4 5 6 7 8 9
A B C D E F G H I

Take a deep breath with your eyes closed and slowly release it. Do it a few times until you feel completely relaxed. You should be feeling exuberant and vibrant. You are striving to stimulate your mental powers. Let us take a moment to quiet things down in our heads with the sole purpose of focusing and reflecting on the thoughts and emotions flowing within us. What are the preconceived idealizations for this exercise? What do you believe its purpose is? When you are done documenting your responses, the final exercise will be comprised of the following:

Do the exact same exercise you just completed, in the exact order. When you are done, do again and again until two minutes have elapsed. Set a timer for two minutes and come to a complete stop at the arrival of two minutes. Once you have fully completed one cycle, continue to do as many as you can within that timeframe.

After the two minutes are up, please summarize your thoughts and emotions as detailed as you can. When you are done, read it aloud, paying attention to how it speaks to you. In that moment, if new or different concepts manifest, embrace them, including them in your personal reflection summary.

Now let us explain the significance and importance of the exercise.

When I posed the first task of signing or printing your name, based on the hundreds of workshops done with this icebreaker, each one of you were able to step into the task without hesitation, resistance, or doubt. You are well-equipped to complete the task. It is something you perform regularly, with confidence in your approach. You were fully cognizant of the outcome.

I would like to emphatically touch the concept of "step into." You want to quickly develop the habit of "step into." You will need to do so in a new way to keep from going back to prison. Master this principle: if you change your thinking, you change the behaviors and, inevitably, you change the outcomes in your life. You will need to step into fatherhood, marriage, a legal paying job—you get the point. Are you committed to the work and make the changes required of you to assure the outcome you aspire?

Remember: you are well-equipped to complete the task. You can perform it with confidence in your approach, fully cognizant of the outcome. You must internalize this by yourself; you must make the decision to believe it. We can enact the same outcomes with our natural and innate abilities, gifts, and talents. Let us identify and define all of the above as your comfort zone.

When the task requested you to rewrite your name with your opposite hand, you felt something preventing you from attacking it rigorously as you did with your dominant hand. What were the barriers, the fears, the doubts compromising your ability to promulgate?

Did you experience shame in some way, based on the silliness of the exercise? Did you give yourself permission to laugh at this? What was your internal dialogue? Was it the same as your external dialogue? Where are you willing to go for something childish or something important like fatherhood or being a husband? Where are you not willing to go or do? Why or why not?

This part of the exercise speaks to our beliefs, our values, and our character. This is where we encounter what we're willing to do and what we will never dare do until we stripped the dysfunctional beliefs within us from all our toxic experiences and rewired our brains to accept the dynamics necessary to change and get better. This is asking you to come out of your comfort zone. You will not find what you need to grow with your old school thinking. To be someone you have never been before requires you do something you have never done before, to go somewhere you have never been before.

The multitask exercise is best defined as working on all your gifts, talents, skills, goals, and time felicitously. Again, when asked to write "multitask," there were no barriers or hesitation. It was easily adhered to and imperiously completed. When the task required you to implement the letter first and then the number, things changed. Finally, when you were executing the exercise to encompass the alphabet letter, things *really* changed. The most important aspect of this exercise was how it slowed you down to perform it. Imagine how much more it would prevent you from staying with the task if you had to do yet another round, as illustrated in chart number three. Here is an example of how far you can become distracted from the things that are important:

```
M  U  L  T  I  T  A  S  K
1  2  3  4  5  6  7  8  9
A  B  C  D  E  F  G  H  I
B  C  D  E  F  G  H  I  J
C  D  E  F  G  H  I  J  K
```

Imagine going on with the above until you reached letter *M.* What type of focus are you operating with? It's extremely difficult to focus on the things that can really make a difference in your life with the distribution of your time on multiple tasks simultaneously. The reality is that there are many hundreds of people living life from this realm. In and out of prison, they have no idea that what they allocate their precious hours of time and life just moves along fine. I learned from a character development class I took with Dr. Shabazz at Otisville Correctional Facility that in every situation we encounter, it is our responsibility to get the lesson so we can graduate to the next lesson in life. The failure to do so does not exempt you from the consequences. Reality will not compensate at that moment of time if you did not get the lesson when you were supposed to.

The multitask portion with the two minutes to conduct as many as time allows speaks of your personal ability to focus, take directions, and execute orders. People engulfed in this way of living have too many distractions to find what it is they really want and what they should be doing. They are sleepwalking throughout their lives. They are the walking dead, zombies. They are unconscious about what's happening and then they reflect, years later, and wonder what the hell happened, and where did those twenty years go?

Now let us be noticeably clear: this exercise is a blah-blah-blah exercise. It is not a life or death exercise. My question to you is, when the minutes concluded, did you come to a full stop? Again, based on the hundreds of workshops I have done, the answer is that some of you did not. That is a clear expression of your real beliefs and values.

Many men and women who have experienced incarceration have the common denominators of not following instructions or rules, or altering them in a way that is conducive to their interpretations of power and controlling the situation. If this is you, I ask you to evoke some time for personal reflection and self-inventory.

I guarantee you, this is not the only area of your life where you will resort to that thinking, attitude, and comfort zone. It is showing up in your relationships, your work, etc.; you are emotionally leaking! If you choose not to confront it, you will go home with this. It will cost you more relationships and could cost you more jobs. Employers will not pay their employees for not following rules, completing instructions, and sticking to tasks. If you work in a construction site and do not adhere to rules, it can cost you your life. Metaphorically speaking, it will cost you your life if you go home with that thinking. It will cost you some more of your life if it takes you back to a world of drugs.

That, in and of itself, will you take right back to prison. You must decide: what do you really want, and what is more important? Do not blame the system, parole, your girl, your boss—it is you! Like an iceberg, components of yourself are at the surface. The tip is expose to the world. The real work, the real you, lies underneath. The core of your values, beliefs, and character is where who you are is stored, where we want to go. It's underneath the surface, deeply embedded in your comfort zone.

VALUES

FROM AGES 1–4 YOU DEVELOP FAMILY VALUES	Derives from words and visions we experienced in areas of family, work, school, success, sex, fun, marriage, religion, honesty, friendship. Anything and everything we experience growing up in the formative years.
FROM AGES 5–9 YOU DEVELOP SOCIAL VALUES	Derives from being taught in school how to act in a crowd, how to walk, when to talk, when to raise our hands and ask for permission, social etiquette.
FROM AGES 10–13 YOU DEVELOP SELF VALUES	Derives from what we believe is important to us from our family values and social values. We lived them out in a way that makes us feel safe, happily avoiding fear.
FROM AGES 14–18 IT'S PARTY TIME	These are the years of experimenting and making dumb decisions, drinking, smoking weed, acting up to dares, and choosing friends based on self-values.
FROM AGES 19–21 EDUCATION	These are the years to be strictly focused on pursuing higher education, training, and certifications. Preparing us to live in preparation of career and establishing a family.

FROM AGES 21–30 FOCUS IS CAREER	These are the years to cultivate your vocation, what you aspire to do for a living, generating an income to do the things that bring you joy, preparing you for family life, allowing adequate savings for retirement.
FROM AGES 30–40 FAMILY	These are the years to develop a family. You're ready to dedicate the time and attention to the important details for a healthy family experience.
FROM AGES 40–60 RETIREMENT	These are the years to allocate the necessary funds allowing you to continue living the lifestyle you are living up until retirement and paying for it easily.
FROM AGES 60–70 OUT OF TIME	If there are any changes necessary to make that will remove something that is stopping you from being able to yield greater peace, joy, happiness, money, and relationships, and you didn't make those changes, you will die a stubborn mule. You will be miserable because you will be all alone.
FROM AGES 70–80 OVERTIME	If you end up in this spectrum, you are truly blessed. Enjoy every moment and every endeavor, with as many people as you can, to the fullest! Share your story.

This chart was a survey conducted by a business program I took at Eastern Correctional Facility in 2004. It was based on the answers in these categories from 200 successful men and women living in Orange County, upstate New York. It deciphers the responses in the chart as a generality elaborating the various stages of development. Most of the individuals surveyed agreed to the findings, outweighing those who did not agree.

In my family value years, my exposure to all these areas of life and more were totally toxic and dysfunctional. Here, within, lay my foundation to life. After growing up in total insanity at the age of five, my introduction to social values was sexual abuse at the age of six. I was further traumatized with the lack of support of my mother, whose response was to slap me, kick me, and pick me up off the floor by my hair. She demanded me to never to speak about it again. I entered the next stage of life with all these contaminated experiences. We are simply not wired to do that; we cannot contain those emotions and experiences without expressing them. In the sixties, the school system was not trained in identifying trauma. Their response was to institute labels on an individual: you're stupid, you have a problem following directions, you're destructive. Here again, my social values were continuing the contamination.

It is easy to see how the formation of my self-values and social values were corrupted. This was what I went through, why I entered the world full of anger, bitterness, confusion, lack of trust, and no respect for self. Therefore, I also had no respect for others, and I was rebellious against authoritative figures.

At the age of thirteen, I stopped going to school. I dropped out. I was in full rage at this point of my life, doing drugs, and no one dared to confront me. I was left alone. Think about that for a moment— thirteen years old, coming in and out of my home when I wanted to and not going to school. The adults living there were so far in their world of insanity and dysfunction that nobody even noticed or cared to address me. Everyone in the house was either consumed with drinking or drugs. Every night was a party night to them. During the day, they were sleeping and recovering from nightly binges. There were absolutely no regards to others or what was happening in the house. I had to take care of myself and my siblings. I was never asked, "Why didn't you go to school today?" Crazy!

At the age of fourteen, I was a father to my premature daughter, Becky. I had her in my life for twenty-two days, and then I had to deal with her death. I had no models for it; I had never experienced the death of someone important to me, and now I had to walk through that valley all alone. This was an additional burden I would need to carry on my own. At the age of twenty-one, I already had three children, experienced two overdoses, and had a juvenile and adult felony record under my belt.

According to the chart, my 20s should have been allocated to the pursuit of education. My 30s should have been the time of my life for contemplating family. From the ages of 13–39, I was a wounded little boy in a man's body, stepping into all these stressful roles. I lacked the emotional wherewithal, the education, and the models I needed. The attributes I could contribute were anger, bitterness, emotional breakdowns, and the other effects of depression. A simple definition for depression is: a hundred miles away from reality! Men that carry a wounded child's mentality are always going to make childish decisions. It is all you know; it is all you have as a foundation.

In my early- to mid-thirties, my brother, son, and father all died. My brother contracted HIV/AIDS and would not stop using heroin, which ultimately consumed him at the age of twenty-eight in 1991. My son, we already know, was selling drugs during the crack explosion years and was shot to death at the age of seventeen in 1993. My father had a heart attack and died at the age of forty-nine in 1992. He struggled with cocaine, drinking and smoking weed. My father and son both died on the same date, March 30th, one year apart. It is easy to see that one of our generational cycles is drugs.

Let us substitute drugs for an actual person and call him an assassin. How many of you would invite this assassin into your home for dinner? That is exactly what I did, in the sense that I continued to do drugs. I did not get the lesson when drugs killed my brother, father, and son. Drugs almost killed me, too, with all the near-death experiences I had.

Drugs will either kill you or take you back to prison. I was not allowed to tell a judge I did not get the lesson. When I needed the lesson to be mastered, it did not make amends to accommodate me with my reality. There are no bright lights in the drug world; that is only the movies.

Finally, I was a grandfather at the age of thirty-three. My oldest daughter was emulating her dad by having a child so young. Here is a question for you: who are you emulating, or would like to emulate? Who would you like your children to emulate, and would you like them to emulate you?

Now, let us correlate these experiences to the chart and let us start with the fun years, 14–18. Party time. I was a dad twice within that time span. I stepped into that role with the declinational self-value system I had accumulated throughout the earlier years. According to the chart, the focus for structuring a family should have been contemplated in my thirties. I was not ready for fatherhood. It is not just based on my age; I was lacking emotional intelligence and the lessons that only evolve toward making comprehensive decisions with my experiences. I made so many mistakes.

I continued the party mentality into my late thirties, when I finally became drug-free. Amid this timeframe, despite the cost to my family by losing so many of the men to the drugs, I never realized that the party boat left when I was eighteen. For another twenty-one years I continued the so-called party. I walked, talked, and acted just like a freaking teenager would all through my twenties, thirties, and early forties.

Here's a true story about my first encounter in my old neighborhood after my release. I learned that many of the guys I used to run with had died, as they had continued to do drugs. The deaths varied from overdose to getting killed in a robbery. More tragically, after fifteen years of not going into my old neighborhood, the ones who were still alive were still doing heroine. They were still hanging out in the same corner, laughing at the same jokes. They were still stuck, living life like it was one big party. They were still numbing their pain and existence in this big world. They were entering their late 50s, approaching their 60s with the same stinking thinking. Alive, but completely dead!

Lastly, I was supposed to finish my education into my twenties, but I dropped out of school at the age of thirteen. I worked as a payroll clerk for a few years in an engineering company. It was a staff of six working in a dark, isolated room. It was an entry-level job, processing timesheets and payroll, where everyone was going home with at least $1,000 a week. We were going home with like, $300. Then, I worked as an accounts payable clerk for a major retail store. Again, I was confined to a corner by myself, working with numbers and paying thousands of dollars in expenses. Then, I did janitorial work, cleaning office buildings. That used to get me sad. Almost everyone had pictures on their desk conveying fun and lovable moments with family. The jobs I held all my life had nothing to do with what I wanted to do. There was nothing empowering, and I really hated going to work. It was all forced on me because of my choices, or lack of choices. I was so freaking miserable, complaining about everything and everyone. I was the victim mentality, personified.

But I didn't do anything to improve my quality of life and I just continued to move from one dead end job to another. I submerged myself deeper into the rat race. Between jobs I was either in rehab or in prison. Each new encounter after being released took me further in a world of hopelessness, depression, anger, and suicidal ideation.

Until, of course, I finally made the decision to do something new so I could become someone new. I dedicated myself to improving my thoughts and my life. I started to practice what I aspired to become every single day.

Here is where the direction of my life took shape.

3

YOUR DOMINANT THOUGHT

Here's an important question: who is the most important person in the world? The answer is you, of course; you are the person you think about. From your perspective, there's no one more important than yourself. Your outlook about yourself defines a statement to those in your circumference.

How you see yourself determines your external world. How important you feel is illuminated in the quality of your relationships. Your self-esteem steers the significance of your goals and strengthens the persistence you evoke when pursuing them.

Let's go back to my narrative of creating E.R.I.C. I was engulfed in a two-year commitment to structure the program. For two years, I worked to figure out how to overcome the objectives. There was plenty of frustration along the way, but I refused to lose.

I was committed until I reached my goal. I had an overflow of all the words and principles you will see throughout the book. I had to learn to say these words every day, and learn what they look like in action.

I finally grasped the discernment of the principle and got the lesson to advance into the next level. It freaking clicked, and I started applying these lessons to every goal I set for myself. I still do this, to this very day. I went from positive knowing to positively believing that if I want it, it is mine.

The more importance you place on yourself, the more significant you become to other people. Your level of reverence is the defining statement in your life. I am going to share some tools, skills, and information about how to become empowered and how to become more important to yourself and other people. You will become more focused and effective in what you do.

Here's a second question: what is the intrinsic value of this book? It is what you do with the abundant stream of material contained in the book. The essential components extracted from this book or anything you learn in life are contained in the specific arrangements of pursuing validity to improve your life.

One of the principles of a goal-setting individual is stepping into fully accomplishing their goals. As you implement these instructions, you will maximize the benefits of attaining optimal results.

The more frequently you act on higher goals, the greater results you will get. As you accumulate better outcomes you will get motivated to continue taking action, to be more, to do more.

You put your life in an upward spiral to greater outcomes. These steps, these principles grant you access to being an active participant in creating your life. You take aim, with full advantage, at every opportunity to live at your fullest potential. The opportunities before you are unlimited. Therefore, your possibilities are endless as well.

Your ability to generate ideas are infinite. This means there is no limit on what you can obtain. There are no limits on what you can have or what you can be. Develop the fire within to expand yourself on a continuous basis. Why are some people more successful than others? Why do they have more money, nicer cars, better houses, better jobs? There are many intricate components to this question. For me, the paradigm shift was thinking, talking, and feeling in every sense that these principles and strategies would alter my outcomes.

I refuse to allow negativity to enter my circumference. Instead, I would inter-connect all the words and principles until they became my default thinking, and then I would act congruently with my new thoughts.

I started to believe in my capabilities to convey a clear message in my life. I believed I was going somewhere. I separated myself from others who had been caught in a cycle of two steps forward, four steps back—sometimes they had been in that cycle for years, even decades.

The Bible says, "seek and you shall find for all who seek it find it." I really did begin to find them. All the answers are at our disposal when we decide to access them. You don't need to reinvent the wheel. Focus on the solutions to a problem. Therewithin, you will find the answer, the people, the plans to confront the matter. Any obstacle can be overcome, any goal can be reached.

I found the law of cause and effect. The Bible says we live in a universe governed by law and order. Everything that happens is for a specific reason, whether we know what that reason is or not. This law states that for every effect in your life there is a specific cause—in other words, nothing happens arbitrarily.

To achieve new horizons there are specific causes, living in happiness has specific causes, and generating wealth has specific causes. Everything you do or fail to do has an effect, positive or negative, somewhere in your life!

The application of cause and effect is this: our thoughts are causes and how we respond to our thoughts with our behaviors are effects. Your thoughts are the cause of the outcomes in your life. Your thoughts are creative; you are creating your life in the manner you see yourself.

This is the fundamental principle to building a greater you. In the Old Testament, it says, "As a man thinketh it in his heart so is he." In the New Testament, it says, "According to his faith it is done unto you."

These are statements that thoughts are the cause of the outcomes in your life. If you want to improve any of the outcomes in your life, improve your thoughts. When you change your thoughts, you will change your behaviors—and, inevitably, the outcomes in your life.

The prognosis for your quality of life is the answer to this question: what's the value of my thoughts and how much time I reside in them? If your thoughts are primarily negative it will be manifested in your life, your relationships, and in your future aspirations.

Thought times emotion equals outcomes. Your thoughts and the amount of time deposited in those thoughts plus how you feel determines your outcomes. If you alter your thoughts, you alter your outcomes. When you think differently, your world begins to adapt accordingly.

Imagine the direction of your thoughts is like driving your car. As you turn the wheel and go down a different road, your outcome—your destination—changes also. As you change your thoughts and go through the mental roads of those striving to reach new limits, everything around you changes, and suddenly, you're reaching the destinations of your desires.

People with dominating positive thoughts think differently from people with dominating negative thoughts. When positive thoughts become the prevailing dominance, you get the positive outcomes. When you begin to drive down the mental road of individuals transitioning from prison triumphantly, you begin to arrive at the same destinations.

This principle is simple, yet many of us miss it, ignore it, or overlook it. We're not cognizant of the work required to ensure our freedom. We strive to reach phenomenal outcomes on the outside without adequately preparing on the inside.

That's sabotaging the law of cause and effect to move us forward. Individuals transitioning successfully focused on thoughts free of incarceration. Individuals transitioning unsuccessfully succumbed to thoughts of imprisonment as the prevailing alternative. A person transitioning successfully talks about goals, hopes, dreams, and future aspirations. These are their dominating thoughts. A person transitioning unsuccessfully contemplates challenges, barriers, parole, people they don't like, their worries, anxiety, their lack of money, their poor health, and all other kinds of problems creating the language and outcomes congruent to the belief that the world is too difficult to navigate. Whatever resides as the prominent thought is what you will experience more of.

Incremental improvement speaks of doubling your income or personal growth by becoming better each day. The Japanese call this the Kaizen Principle. It means "continuous betterment."

First, you must decide to improve productivity, performance, and output by a small amount every day. You can get better by 0.1 percent each day. That equates to 0.5 percent in five business days. Less than one percent!

If you become better 0.5 percent each week for four weeks, you become 2 percent more productive by the end of the month. There are thirteen four-week months in every year (to compensate the difference between short months versus longer months). If you become 2 percent better every four weeks, at the end of the year you will become 26 percent more productive in the essential areas of your life. This kind of growth will never take you back to prison or drugs. Is not going back to prison your most dominating thought?

Any incremental growth and improvement in one area affects other areas of your life. Your dedication to work this principle will make you 26 percent better, all around, at the end of each year. You will become twice as productive in two years. By becoming 0.1 percent better, you elevate your performance 26 percent each year and will *double* your income every 2.5 to 3 years. This gives you a compass to improving your life.

Work as quickly as possible to enhance your performance, productivity, and output. Once you decide to start, latch on like a pit bull and don't let go. Do not stop the momentum.

Learn how to set goals and manage your time more efficiently.

It will trigger the law of cause and effort to your advantage. You can immediately start to grow, drastically elevating your output. Whatever you accomplish in one week, you can accomplish another week. Do this for four weeks straight and you create the habit of developing personal growth. These principles work if you work!

Master these laws of change to start building your foundation.

THE LAW OF BELIEF

Whatever you accept as true will combine with emotions to become your reality. The more emotion supporting your belief, the faster it comes for you. Your beliefs cause you to see the world despite the way it really is. Just because you see the world your way does not mean it is reality. All improvement comes when you determine to modify your beliefs in specific areas of your current reality—especially if we're aspiring to eradicate addiction or incarceration.

You don't believe what's before you; instead, you see what you already believe. Start to believe you are destined for greatness. If you believe with confidence that you will become successful, your belief will produce this in your reality. If you believe you will be great, you will take the necessary action to line yourself up accordingly for greatness.

Ignore all the barriers. Sprout yourself ahead after every impediment in your life. If you believe success is guaranteed, nothing will stop you from actualizing the outcome. The reason many of us under-achieve is because we're dominated with negative thoughts and outcomes. We believe ourselves to be limited in some way. We believe we're not smart enough, we don't have enough money, we're not creative enough, not deserving enough. Some of us undermine our talents or other forms of deficiencies. Some people want to wait until the time is right—which, by the way, never comes. The time is *always* right; just start!

If you think people are more worthy than you are, you inadvertently declare that you are worth less. You unconsciously conclude you're less-than. You're as smart as you grant yourself the permission to be. Learned to use the law of cause and effect to abstract optimal outcomes.

I started by reading books and audio programs. I started by taking courses. I learned cause and effect for my goals and then applied it. I began to dress in my mind as if I were living, in the moment, as an entrepreneur walking down the business district in New York City. I would imagine and see myself dressed in a suit while in a cell at a maximum-security prison, believing in my heart that it was just a matter of time. When I got home, I got the opportunity to play it exactly the way I practiced it. I was strolling through downtown Wall Street, in a board meeting, at a fundraiser, dressed in some awesome suits. Mentally, I was thousands of miles away from prison where I cultivated the vision. I started to talk the jargon; my thoughts were fully amplified. I walked the walk and talked the talk, and in essence, I became what I believed. Why? Because this is all I thought about, all the time.

I read everything of substance, nothing frivolous. I stopped reading books of frivolous substance and read instead about character development, leadership, business, real estate, banking, credit, the Federal Reserve System, the economy, finance, relationships, how to be a dad, and how to be a husband.

These books are readily available in the greatest institution of the world, New York State Department of Corrections, and every other state in this country! There are no barriers to the library inside a prison except for the ones we create.

Each book yielded me twenty to forty years of the author's experience. I was reading a book a week; at the end of the year, I had amassed fifty-two books times the years of the authors' experience. I believe with all my heart these authors were my mastermind team.

The content in my book derives from biblical principles, personal experiences, training, education, and reading. Collectively, these attributes inspired the strategies I evoked. I currently follow everything these giants put out: Rick Warren, Brian Tracey, Steve Covey, Napoleon Hill, John Allan, Norman Vincent Peale, John Maxwell, Tony Robbins, Robert Kiyosaki, Joel Osteen, Tim Keller, and my old Pastor from New York City, Pete Scazzero, and his wife, Gerri Scazzero to name a few.

The way to change your life instantly, reaching new horizons, is this: stop watching TV, playing video games, and hanging out with negative people, and instead, read, read, read! Neurotic people will say and do neurotic things. Don't justify their behaviors and believe what you see.

THE LAW OF EXPECTATIONS

This law states whatever you expect with a firm belief becomes your self-fulfilling prophecy. You will not achieve what you want, but you achieve what you expect. Your expectations exert an enormous influence on you and the people around you. If you anticipate being popular, you will be. If you expect to make sales, you will be one of the top salespersons in your company. If you expect to find your potential, this will inevitably become your self-fulfilling prophesy. Do you expect to be jail-free and drug-free?

Your expectations define your attitude. If you expect things will turn out well, you will have a positive attitude. You will assert a positive attitude on others; they will be more inclined to working with you. Successful people are constantly exhibiting and expressing positive expectations to others. In prison, individuals with a negative connotation are walking time bombs. Who wants to be near a person like that?

What are your conversations sounding like? Are your thoughts about outcomes exemplifying things you desire? Identify expectations by listening to yourself and your internal dialogues.

THE LAW OF ATTRACTION

You attract the people and circumstances that are in harmony with your dominant thoughts. The more intense emotions you invoke with your words, thoughts, and mental pictures, the quicker you attract similar ideas, people, resources, and opportunities into your life.

Prior to starting E.R.I.C. in Otisville Correctional Facility, I applied this principle and mastered it in the moment. I was able to ascertain the participation of civilians contributing their time to the mission. I had real estate brokers, bankers, lawyers, contractors, mortgage brokers, and investors coming into the facility to formalize the program. They were able to give the program creditability with their presence, assuring I wasn't freestyling with the curriculum.

Do you understand how difficult this was for me to accomplish while incarcerated? I refused to accept I couldn't overcome the barriers in my way. This outcome taught me, if I can accomplish this in prison, there's nothing stopping me when I got home.

Everything you have in your life today you have attracted to yourself because of the person you are. You can understand now how easy it is to change your life. You can change your thoughts and, inevitably, the person you are. You can change the way you think and begin attracting new people and circumstances into your life.

THE LAW OF CONCENTRATION

Whatever thoughts you populate grow in your life. The more you induce thoughts about something and the more you provoke these thoughts with emotions, the more those thoughts ascend. Eventually they will dominate all your other thoughts. What resides in your mind?

Do you constantly reflect upon the goals you want to achieve? Do you focus on possibilities, hope, and creating an ideal future? Can you envision yourself free from drugs and prison? Do you deposit thoughts on the people you love? What amount of time are you allocating to your dominant thoughts? The answer determines the quality of your life.

THE LAW OF HABIT

Ninety-five percent of your daily activities derives from your habits. You can learn new habits that are consistent with the life you aspire toward. Good habits are hard to sculpt but easy to rest in. Bad habits are easy to develop but problematic to live with. I propose you start to decide on the habits most conducive to securing your freedom. Then, embark on developing those habits until they become your dominant thoughts.

Give these thoughts ownership and a permanent address in your mind; think about these habits throughout your entire day. The keys to successfully transition from prison are simple: learn good habits and make them your wife. Once you implement a new habit, you get better outcomes. Anything you practice for twenty-one days consecutively becomes a habit. Start with a ritual every morning focusing on your agenda for the important task of the day. At the end of the month, you will have mastered the habit of working on priorities that elevate you toward continued growth.

THE LAW OF SUBCONSCIOUS ACTIVITY

Your subconscious mind is a powerful computer making all your thoughts and behaviors fit a pattern consistent with your self-conception. Once you activate a thought into your subconscious mind, it initiates adjustment in your behavior to produce the arrival of that thought.

Think and talk about what you want. Activate your subconscious mind to work on what you want, twenty-four hours a day. Your subconscious mind can assist you or destroy you, depending on what you feed it. It functions automatically; it acts on whatever thoughts you hold, evoking the emotion of desire or fear. You can inverse any fear by regulating thoughts in harmony with your desires. Some of us who have experienced addiction or incarceration, whether physically or mentally, struggle with this ideology. This is an area you will be required to tune into everyday if you are going to take charge of the new direction in your life.

Here, you are circumventing fear, which is a summary of your past. Simultaneously you are instituting new habits into your subconscious mind. At the crossroad of change your past will attempt to take control of the future. You will encounter your comfort zone every time you require changing something from that past.

Whenever you want something intensely, think about it. Visualize it. Your subconscious will then go into high gear to manifest it into existence.

THE LAW OF CORRESPONDENCE

Your external world is a mirror image of your internal world. Every area of your life—how much money you make, your standard of living, your health—are reflections of the way you see these things on the inside. As you transpose your thoughts and the rebuilding on the inside, you cultivate your reality externally. Your external always reflects your internal. Each of these thoughts and outcomes are learnable through practice. As you formulate these thoughts you begin to get empowered as you embark on your personal journey.

FUTURE THOUGHTS AND FOCUS

Continuously focus on the future and where you're going rather than the past and what you left behind. There is an enormous gap of individuals thinking about future orientation. People are stuck in their comfort zones thinking about the past. They think about the mistakes they've made and the regrets they have. When they are caught in the moment it is only because they're thinking about immediate gratification and having fun in the short term.

Only a small group purposely have a view about the future and determining their destination. Here's a simple measurement to test future thinking. Ask yourself where you intend to be in one, three, and five years. Future thinkers have clear, specific, written goals and plans for the ensuing years before them. Past-orientation people have no idea at all what's next in life. The better you think out your future, the better outcomes you will receive in the present. Act today to make your desired future a reality. Administer your long-term forecast with a short-term purview. Cultivating long-term goals converts you to a future-minded perspective.

SETTING GOALS

Become clear about what you want. When you establish clear goals, follow up immediately with the details to achieve it in writing. Be sure to review, every single day the next steps in the endeavor. To be able to set goals and make plans for their attainment is a must-have skill in your toolbox.

RESULT-FOCUSED OUTCOMES

Set clear priorities on your daily tasks. Concentrate working on the best use of your time with emphasis on the one thing that propels you most. What's the most essential task in the moment?

SOLUTION-FOCUSED

Manipulate your thoughts into finding solutions instead of problems. Stay rooted in concentrating on what can be done rather than what happened and who did it. You can pivot your thoughts from negative to positive by taking your thoughts away from your problems, focusing on solutions. When you endure adversity in your life—and you will—I suggest you pose the question: what's the solution? What can I do, what's the next step, where can I go from here, what can I learn from the situation to make me smarter while moving toward my desired future?

Seek and you shall find—these are the lessons in adversity to get better. Challenges come to instruct, not to obstruct. Look for the nuggets of wisdom, no matter the situation. Every obstacle contains the seed to a greater advantage, so be determined to find it. Develop the habit of being solution-focused. As your thoughts continue to evolve, while seeking solutions, you start to guarantee greater outcomes.

ACHIEVING EXCELLENT OUTCOMES

Become determined to excel at whatever you step into, even if it's temporary. The market pays immense compensation for optimal performance. It pays average dollars for average outcomes and pennies for below-average outputs of labor. To be proficient at what you do, you must produce high self-worth. You will ultimately start to feel like a winner internally, and you will overflow equally externally. This will determine the level of respect you receive from people around you.

RELATIONSHIPS

To fortify optimal contentment in your personal and business endeavors, relationships are enormously important. Diligently make every effort to establish quality relationships, especially with the important people in your family and professional circles. Your happiness and unhappiness are reciprocated from the relationships you have. If you're currently in a toxic relationship, get out, NOW! If you don't, in the end you will lose yourself and the relationship. Is it worth it? Absolutely not. Happiness is crucial for the arrival of your greatest aspirations.

ACTION-ORIENTED

Imagine yourself like a horse, feeling anxious at the gate to sprint for the ultimate victory of your life. You're constantly moving into your goals. Have the sagacity to resolve priorities. Develop an exuberant appetite for action and adjourn whatever is contrary. No fast foods, no shortcuts, no excuses, and no procrastinating.

Below are seven disciplines that are significant for the new you.

The first is goal setting. People driven by clear goals act congruent with their attainment every day, in every circumstance that contributes to the goal, and with the people who support the exertion.

The second is time management. This requisite petitions you to converge your days into blocks of hours or half-hours. It is the only currency to manage your time effectively. You must pay for it in advance with deliberate intent and focus.

The third is balance. This requires you to find the proper balance between family and work in advance.

The fourth is good health. This means you take care of your physical health exceptionally well or better.

The fifth is continuous learning. Make an allegiance to personal development. This is essential for how high you rise. Learning does not mean you must attend college. Remember, the best university in the world is The Department of Corrections Library. Read books, order books. In the free world, the best university is also the library, with its massive selections—in conjunction with YouTube and Google. You can learn anything you need to learn without going to college, if you prefer.

The sixth is finance. To progress financially on any magnitude, build with a long-term focus ideology. Suzie Orman, a professional advisor, wrote about the law of money. It states, "take care of your money and whenever you need it, money will take care of you."

The seventh is integrity. Character regulates the quality of relationships in your life, both personally and in business.

To wrap up, you're valuable and important to yourself and to the people you affect. You have untapped potential. You can create your world as you desire. Create your world by the thoughts and depth of your convictions. You are free to feel the context of your thoughts, and therefore, the direction of your life.

There are no restraints to what you can do, be, or have—except for the boundaries *you* create. Your outcomes get better when you get better. It does not matter where you're coming from. All that matters is where you are going. Where you're going is regulated by your imagination. You're only as free as your options, as the alternatives you have available at any given time. The more options you erect in your personal and business life, the greater outcomes you will have.

With every difficulty, there's a seed for a greater outcome. Your obligation should be to find it. You can achieve any goal you set for yourself. The only things preventing this are the self-limitations you impose.

4

YOUR BELIEF SYSTEM

In the middle of my transformation, I concluded that if I expect new and better outcomes in my life, I must reconstruct my thoughts and belief system. If I want life to get better, I must get better at how I see the world.

I learned how to maximize my potential yielding the appropriate return on investment in Self Inc. Immediately after implementing these strategies, my life improved. I eventually went from rags to riches with my thoughts actively engaging the ensuing principles. The following strategies illuminate a comprehensive outline to enhance your development. You can optimize your abilities to absorb information and apply it accordingly. I guarantee you, these principles work if you work. They will tap into your potential. To the degree you want it, see it, taste it—to that degree, it will be yours.

Unlike a rubber band, when you stretch your mind to a new plateau by acquiring knowledge, your mind should never retract to its original position prior to obtaining that knowledge. That would only place you in the same position as if you never ascertained new information. Stretch your mind and imagine yourself becoming the person you always wanted to be. You have all the potential to do something special in life. The question you should be thinking about right now is, will you?

We're all born with unique gifts. However, a lot of us start out with mediocre talents. Individuals achieving peak outcomes do it by developing natural talent and abilities to a high degree.

An awesome measure of potential is expressed in the equation:

$$IA + AA \times A = IHP$$

IA is for inborn attributes. Your disposition, characteristics, and mental capacity to overcome barriers.

AA is acquired attributes. Your knowledge, problem solving skills, and abilities acquired throughout your experiences in life, maturing the critical areas of emotional intelligence.

A is your attitude. The spirit or energy you contribute on the combination of inborn and acquired attributes.

IHP stands for individual human performance.

The formula is, inborn attributes plus acquired attributes, multiplied by your attitude, equals your individual human performance.

The quality and quantity of attitude can be ascended without resistance. An individual with average inborn attributes and average acquired attributes can still perform at peak performance, so long as a positive attitude is exhibited. It's your attitude more than your aptitude that determines your performance. A positive attitude in this context is defined in the way you respond to adversity. The way you can identify the kind of attitude you default to is how you respond when things get crazy.

Your attitude is distinguished by your anticipation of how things will evolve. If you anticipate good outcomes, you will have a positive attitude. What you believe will happen will produce your attitude, positive or negative. Your expectations are determined by your beliefs about yourself and your world.

If you have a positive worldview, you believe the world is perfect and, in essence, you fit perfectly. You will have the tendency to anticipate the prominent outcomes for yourself, from others and from the situations that come your way.

Your positive affirmation is expressed as a positive mental attitude. The people in your circumference will reciprocate the attitude you expressed. The value of your beliefs determine the substance of your personality.

Self-concept is the bundle of thoughts you sculpt for yourself and the world you see. It's your subconscious. Your beliefs determine your reality. Your external world is a true reflection of your internal world. You actively participate in your world through the vison formed by your belief structure. Your self-concept can predict your outcomes by the deposits you make. You will act in a manner congruent with the many beliefs you've acquired. There is a direct correlation with your level of effectiveness and your self-concept. You could never execute at a more significant level than the perception of your ability to implement it. Your subconscious is subjective; it is based on elucidations you have absorbed about yourself and embraced as authentic.

Remember the chart about family values, social values, and self-values we discussed? When your self-concept in an area is lacking, it derives from an erroneous summary. It's created on self-limiting thoughts you have accepted as accurate. You then act in agreement with the belief. I took on the dysfunctional values presented to me growing up because it came from people that were damaged in some way. That was all they had to give. Every adult member in my family either drank alcohol or did drugs. From early childhood on, any debate or situation deemed disrespectful led to violence. I remember when I was about ten years old getting beat —my mother sent me back with the broomstick and demanded I hit him with it. I was scared to death of my mom, so I broke the broom on this kid. The information I was given was faulty, but I accepted it at face value. I had no other models to emulate, therefore I lived life with limited options.

You have a synopsis statement of your beliefs. You also have a collection of insubordinate self-concepts controlling your performance and behavior in areas you consider to be important.

You have a self-concept for how you look, how you express yourself, how smart|you feel you are or not. You have a self-concept in parenting, how popular you are, how you play sports. If you're in sales, you have a self-concept for how good you think you are as a salesperson, how good you are at objections, how good you are at closing.

You have a self-concept for how you manage your time or not. You will outline the value perceived in these self-concepts and profusely surrender obedience accordingly.

You have self-concept for income you feel capable of obtaining. You can never earn more or less than your self-concept level of income. If you earn 10 percent above or below you immediately engage in compensatory behaviors.

If you earn 10 percent too much you begin to find ways and reasons to buy and spend the money. This occurs when someone is in possession of more money than what is consistent with their self-concept. If you earned 10 percent below you intensified with scrambling behaviors. You focus on innovative ways to create additional income, to work longer. You start to contemplate new job opportunities to get back to your comfort level of income.

Quickly, answer this question: how much money do you need to generate to sustain and manage your way of living comfortably? Go as high as it makes you feel comfortable. Inevitably, you will go to an extreme and start to feel it is not possible for you to generate that kind of income. Your self-concept level of income is called your comfort zone. As it relates monetarily, individuals resist to depart from their zones. Upon feeling firmly secure in that zone, every effort to maintain the status quo is instituted. This striving for consistency or staying in a comfort zone is called homeostasis.

The natural propensity is to resist any deviation, even a positive approach, that feels like a departure from your comfort zones. Comfort zones breed habits and habits propagate ruts. You are in full possession of all the intellect, innovation, and courage you need to withdraw the minute you make the decision to remove yourself from the insanity you prefer to justify and rationalize, making your ruts more accommodating. Think about when you contemplated switching jobs—what were the internal conversations holding you back?

Self-concept is made up of three parts. The first is your self-ideal. This is the description of the person you aspire to be. This vision of your possible future asserts an influence on your behavior. This ideal is a combination of all the qualities and attributes you admire.

High performing and achieving individuals have clear self-ideals. They're constantly striving toward them. The more unambiguous you are about who you want to be, the higher the likelihood you will evolve into that person. You will ascend to the standards of your admiration, your dominant aspiration.

Individuals that struggle to advance have an incoherent self-ideal or have no self-ideal at all. They exude little or no thought to pronounce the person they desire to be. Because they give no thought to it, their evolution slows down and they get stuck in a mental rut, residing there for years or even decades.

The second part of your self-concept is your self-image. Your self-image is how you see yourself. Your thoughts about yourself are shown externally in your actions, which means your actions are consistent with the scope you hold of yourself on the inside. Your self-image is your inner mirror which tells you how you're supposed to function in a situation.

The third part of your self-concept is your self-esteem. Your self-esteem is how you feel about yourself, the emotional component of your personality. It is the foundation to happiness, to personal growth. Your height of self-esteem is how valuable and competent you feel. Each one reinforces the other. When you feel good about yourself you perform well. When you perform well you feel good about yourself.

Self-esteem is how you like yourself. Whatever thoughts you hold constantly will become your reality. If you constantly assert how much you love yourself, your self-esteem will be the sum total of that assertion.

The abundance of loving yourself will demand you to do more and therefore become more. The greater you love yourself, the greater your level of confidence. The more positive your outlook, the healthier and happier you will be. Individuals with high self-esteem are peak performers and high achievers.

You cannot be dependent on the feedback, criticism, love, comments, or acceptance of another person to feel alive. You must love yourself with the best love you have available.

It is through loving yourself to this degree that you tell others how you want and need to be loved without ever saying a word. It reaffirms to others that you will not accept any words or behaviors that are out of balance with the above summary. Remember, you cannot give to another what you are lacking in self.

Going back to my introduction, I elaborated how I never heard the words "I love you." Since I did not hear the words "I love you" growing up, there was no way for me to convey it in action. I never saw it, therefore I had no clue the impact it had on me. During my transformational endeavor, I had to repeat "I love myself" hundreds of times before it was fully internalized. It was then that I was able to accept I am loveable. Through that love came joyful moments and living in peace with myself. When I lived out these truths, I was finally able to experience love. You must love yourself first and, through that loving, express to others how it is you want to be loved. As a bonus, you will no longer tolerate not receiving love in the manner you need. You are no longer dependent to do well based on the distribution of love from another person.

There are two rules regarding self-esteem. Number one: you can never like or love anyone else more than you like or love yourself. You can't give away what you don't have. Rule number two: you can never expect anyone else to like, love, or respect you more than you like, love, or respect yourself. Your own level of self-liking and self-esteem is the control valve on your relationships. It is the problem or the solution.

Everything you do to stimulate your level of self-esteem will improve and enlarge your level of satisfaction and happiness. Where does your self-concept come from? No one is born with a self-concept. Everything you believe about yourself you have learned from all your experiences, positive or negative, since infancy. Each child comes into the world as pure potential—with a temperament and certain inborn attribute, yes, but no self-concept at all.

Every attitude, behavior, value, opinion, belief, and fear has been learned. If there are elements of your self-concept that don't align with your purposes, you can eradicate them. Understanding how your self-concept is formed is possible. Doing so will bring the changes that will make you the person you want to be. Become the person who can accomplish goals that are important.

It is fear that steals our happiness. Is fear causing us to settle for less. Fear is the root cause of negative emotions and unhappiness. The fear I'm describing here is in relevance to growing and doing things that push us to be more in life. There are moments when fear serves us well and protects us. Looking out of a 20th floor window is scary to me, and that fear tells me if I fall out of the window I'm probably going to die. If I'm in Yankee stadium sitting at the very top deck and needed to use the restroom, as I descended toward the platform to the men's room, fear tells me to be extremely cautious going down the steep stairway. The only good thing about fear is that it is learned. Therefore, it can be unlearned.

The fear of failure and the fear of rejection are learned responses, programmed in our infancy years. Fears set the height of our upper and lower limits of our comfort zones. If you do enough not to be criticized or rejected on the low side you will avoid risk or failure on the high side. When you established your comfort zone, you stayed there to avoid feelings of fear or anxiety. The good news is you can unlearn fears. You can consistently eradicate them from your arsenal. If you do, everything you want becomes available.

The opposite of fear is love, starting with self-love. There is an inverse relationship between self-esteem and fear of all kinds. The more you love yourself the less you fear failure and rejection. The more you love yourself the more willing you are to on take risk, leading to greater outcomes.

Happiness can move you out of your comfort zone. You can raise your self-esteem, overriding your fears by repeating, with emotion and conviction, the powerful words of "I love myself" over and over. Say it ten, fifty, or one hundred times a day until it locks into your self-conscious. You will begin to feel the difference in your confidence, competence, and relationships.

Here is a powerful exercise. Finish the following statement with as many answers you can think of: if I were totally unafraid of anything or anyone, what I would do differently in my life? Finish that statement with as many answers as possible. When you carefully sit down to write these answers, you will learn two things. First, you will learn what a big role fear plays in your life. Second, you will catch a glimpse of the possibilities you will be able to do once you have unlearned your fears. Develop the quality of unwavering courage and self-confidence.

5

THE POWER OF YOUR MIND

Your subconscious mind is powerful. When used effectively, it can move you forward to the destination of your desire. Your subconscious can be used for innovative endeavors or annihilation, for kindness or evil. It embarks you to victory or failure based on the calibration of your thoughts and the specific commands you instill into them. To conform your potential, learn how to regulate access into your subconscious mind for your purposes.

Learn to manipulate your subconscious and conscious mind in harmony. Imagine the size of a head on a newborn baby and the size of an adult with a huge head standing side by side. This visualization represents the comprehensiveness of your conscious and subconscious mind. The baby's head is your conscious mind, and the adult's huge head is your subconscious. The two minds are unequivocally fundamental but have distinctive functions. The conscious mind is the unbiased mind. It has no recollection, holding one thought at a time. This mind has four functions.

1. Identification of information. This information derives from the five senses: sight, hearing, smell, taste, and touch.

2. Information you see and hear is instantly conveyed to your subconscious mind for comparison with all previous experiences in similar encounters. Based on those experiences, the subconscious mind scrutinizes imminent danger for a fight or flight response.
3. An analysis of the events, words, people, etc.
4. The making of a decision. Your conscious mind accepts or rejects the data in the analysis stage, requiring you to decide. It only holds one thought at a time, positive or negative, agreement or disagreement, justified or not justified.

Once you mandate a directive, the conscious mind promptly fulfils your command. Your subconscious mind is a memory bank. The primary objectives are to preserve and recuperate data synchronizing your words and action into the thoughts stipulating the commandment. Your subconscious mind is subjective. It doesn't think conventionally. It will always conform to the command instituted from your conscious mind.

The conscious mind instructs, and the subconscious mind becomes subservient. The subconscious mind is submissive, occupied with the required diligence for producing the necessary behavior and thoughts. Your subconscious can deliver you into riches or poverty according to your habitual mode of thoughts.

The subconscious mind plays in the mental realm of subjugating your thoughts and acting consistently with your past. All your habit patterns are found in your subconscious mind. Your subconscious mind memorizes your comfort zones, striving to keep you buried there.

Absenteeism of clear instructions from your conscious mind to your subconscious mind will control the emotional and physical attributes of your comfort zone, creating comfortability when you deviate from your established patterns of thought and behavior, even at the expense of moving in the direction of your desired goals. Take a moment to read that again, and reflect on that thought, please.

Your subconscious is keeping you on track, according to the input and instructions you programmed into it. There are several laws controlling all the activities in your subconscious mind.

1. **Law of Subconscious Activity.** Any concept accepted as true in your conscious mind is undertaken as a command by your subconscious mind. Your subconscious mind will promptly commence to produce it into your reality. When I stopped doing drugs, applying this principle help me to abdicate twenty-six years of mental poison preventing me to abstain from drugs. Individuals that attempt to quit using drugs struggle with the constant bombardment of thoughts and reasons to get high again. You said to yourself, "just this one time," which, by the way, never happens. When you go back "just this one time," you embark on another relapse. You come up with thoughts like, "I can perform better at work," "I can cope better with the difficult situations we encounter in life," "I can party better," and "I can be more engaged in social events," but none of those excuses are true.

2. **Law of Concentration.** Whatever your dominant thoughts are, they grow exponentially. An increase of positive thoughts will induce the probability of producing positivity in your reality. When you populate anything positive or negative, you transmit a command for your subconscious mind to assign more capacity of your mental powers, bringing that into your life. Renew your thoughts and jargon about what it is you want. Otherwise, you will continue to magnetize the thoughts and words that has netted you the outcomes in your life today. What are the words and thoughts you give life to? While in recovery from my drug addiction I perpetually focused on sobriety. The instant the thoughts of

getting high surfaced I pivoted my thoughts to being sober and what it feels like to live life from this realm. Initially it was a constant battle to control these thoughts, but I was committed to achieving my desired result.

3. **Law of Substituion** is substituting one thought for another. Remember, the conscious mind can only hold one thought at any given time. You can abolish negative thoughts from your conscious mind by substituting them with a positive thought. This mental control enables you to change your thoughts to something positive. Thinking about a solution is inherently positive and it causes you to be calm quickly. Focusing your thoughts on someone you care about, or a pending vacation, is an example of substituting thoughts.

4. **Law of Habit** refers to transforming the inner attitude of mind. By doing so, you change the outer aspect of life. The obstacles between you and evolving into what you desire are your comfort zones. Everything you are and everything you do descends from your habits. The law of inertia says a body in motion tends to remain in motion unless acted upon. The mental definition says in the absence of a definitive effort on your part, you will continue doing, saying, and thinking the same things indefinitely. You'll work in the same way, you'll relate to the same people and get the same reactions from them as you've done in the past, you'll eat the same foods, engage in the same activity. You'll earn the same money, spend the same amount of time on development, and live in the same kind of house in the same neighborhood driving the same car. Using the same example of conflict with my thoughts regarding my desire to be drug-free, it was extremely difficult controlling

my thoughts in the beginning. It was the repetition of changing my thoughts that cultivated the habit, assuring I would be triumphant with the achievement of my goal.

Changing your habits is extremely difficult. You have certain habits that need to be abandoned and others that are critical for your development. Self-mastery, self-control, and self-discipline are essential habits you must implement if you truly aspire to be drug- and jail-free. In aggregating thoughts and actions repeatedly and frequently, you generate a new habit. From here, you can construct any habit you desire. You can activate the person you yearn to be if you will discipline yourself to act in a way that is consistent with your highest ideal, long enough, and hard enough for them to become new habits of thought and behavior.

1. **Law of Emotion.** Your decisions are based on emotions. Every decision you make is determined by the dominant emotion you're experiencing at that time. The two emotions imperative to comprehend due to how they impact our behavior are fear and desire. Fear is the essence of our negative thinking and outcomes. The greater our thoughts and behaviors are deprived of fear, the more pronounced our outcomes will be.

Exploiting the law of substitution to stimulate thoughts of desired outcomes will moderate your thoughts of fear. Thoughts you inhabit compound, like interest, accordingly. Your goal now would be to implement full concentration of this principle, submerging only on the outcomes you aspire toward. Remember, the conscious mind only has sufficient space for one thought at any given time. If you maximize your time with deliberate thoughts on the outcomes and your desires, by the principle of omitted alternatives, you no longer find yourself allocating time on outcomes you fear.

Socrates once said, "to get to Mount Olympus just be sure every step takes you there." In other words, to generate optimal outcomes (walking to your own Mount Olympus), invest your thoughts into that direction without deviation or procrastination.

The outcomes you aspire toward begin to arrive with the daily access of capitalizing your power of choice, in other words, taking systematic control over the thoughts you place in your conscious mind. By rigorously disciplining your thoughts and jargon about what you aspire toward and repudiating outcomes you seek to eradicate, you will enter into the galaxy and see the stars.

Some of our habitual activities and dialogues generate from a low level of awareness. We become subjugated as if in a mental cloud, having demised recollection. This preoccupied state is deliberately circumventing reflection on crucial parts of our lives we would rather not deal with. Inevitably it becomes our default thinking. We fail to acknowledge this, going through the motion for years, even decades. We only become conscious provisionally by the shock of difficult events that shake us to the core. As we regain composure, we tumble back into a waking consciousness where our thoughts flow like collages.

To ascertain all you can be, it's imperative to amplify alertness, becoming fully aware and fully awake. Learn to operate control over your thoughts, empowering the mental laws to navigate your own choosing rather than steering you blindly. Start the process of awakening by reflecting on your life in the future.

Instead of viewing yourself in the negative encounters of the past as a victim, begin to see yourself as an active participant in your evolution. To evolve to a higher plateau, understand: all your past experiences are part of a greater purpose. Every event in your life is an integral part of your purpose. Undertake your current situation as exactly what you need in this moment to indoctrinate something you need to continue an upward spiral for the next lesson in your life. In this context, see every experience as a positive experience. In viewing an opportunity for elevation, you raise the scope of your self-worth.

Now project backward, with calmness and positive thoughts, on how all your experiences were prevalent in your timeline. They were necessary. They were designed to instruct you in some way, embarking you forward into the many possibilities available for you.

The outcomes in your life could not have come into fruition in any other way, especially if you were predominately operating on autopilot.

Stand back and develop a holistic perspective of the complex linkage of events bringing you to where you are right now. You will impose on your experiences a sense of coherence.

The feeling that your life is part of something bigger than yourself enraptures the "everything happens for a reason" way of thinking perfectly. As you view the outcomes in your life as a series of events conspiring toward you achieving what awaits you, you develop a sense of destiny, which is the emblem of your fullest potential and purpose.

This simple ideology in self-awareness enables you to unlock the powers of your choosing to view yourself as an active creator in your life. You take mental control, placing your hands firmly on your own destiny. From there, you determine your future. You free yourself from the law of accident, effectuating your own thoughts and directing the outcomes in your life. Things won't happen randomly anymore. You actuate the causes and effects, reflecting the coincidences that have shaped you into the person you are.

You see, nothing happens arbitrarily. Everything happens with purpose and is happening right now because of an immutable law, even if you cannot see where your life is going. You triggered the law of belief when you accepted your life, and your experiences are leading you toward the accomplishment of something important. The quicker you submerge your thoughts in the eventuality of you already being in possession of your goals, the quicker it will arrive for you. Your beliefs do become your reality. This self-expectancy converts your life into happy outcomes.

Your expectations create your own self-fulfilling prophecy. Your positive future thoughts ignite the switch to the law of attraction, drawing the people and circumstances in harmony with the dominant thoughts. As you value your thoughts in a high regard, you will start to appreciate all the unique blessings you possess and receive.

As you plant seeds of positive thoughts and outcomes into your conscious mind, continually holding them, your subconscious begins to make all your words, feelings, and actions—even your body language—fit a pattern consistent with your new self-concept and your new goals.

Use the law of substitution with the knowledge that your main objective is to keep thoughts of fear, anger, and self-doubt out. Focus on holding thoughts of faith, hope, and love until firmly rooted with a heartbeat. Work with the law of emotion, keeping your thoughts on what you desire. Develop your new attitude by constant repetition, producing a new habit.

Take time each day to soak your mind in positivity and uplifting thoughts, remembering that what you focus on with an abundancy of time will eventually materialize in your reality.

Be patient, calm, and trusting. You *will* achieve what you are meant to achieve, when you are ready for it. When you are fully prepared. Remember, whatever you want also wants you! Whatever you want is traveling right at you. Your primary aim is to get out of your own way.

After seeing the new, positive, and constructive way of seeing your life—a greater and in-depth view of past, present, and future—anchor yourself to these principles. Expound a prominent approach of creating positive thoughts. Harmonize with these mental laws, and your life will accelerate. You will become more alert, aware, and awake. Put yourself onto the high road of maximum performance.

Take a piece of paper and make a list of everything you want in your life. Happiness, health, good friends, prosperity, true financial success, recognition, the respect of others, etc. Let your imagination run freely. The second part is a test. For the next twenty-four hours, think and talk about things on your list. See if you can get through with one day without criticizing, condemning, complaining, getting angry, getting upset, or worrying about anything. If you can do it for one day, there is no reason why you would not be able to do it for two, unless you choose to quit and run back to your comfort zone. If you maintain a momentum of two days, you can do a week, then two weeks, then three weeks. You just cultivated new essential habits to guarantee your new life!

You have now erected the inner strength and strength of character needed to create positive thoughts, which will deliver what you want in life. This exercise will give you real insight about where you are into your development, and it will also show you how far you must go.

The stuff that's found in the middle is what you need to work on to get from one day to one week, from one week to one month, from one month to one year, from one year to the life you yearn for. I promise you, *these principles work if you work*. If you change your thinking, you will change the behaviors, and with that, the outcomes in your life.

6

THE RESPONSIBLE ADULT

To become great, you must accept complete responsibility for who you are. You cannot place blame on anyone or anything. It was not Mommy's fault, it was not the system's fault, it was not bad breaks, it was not because of your race, your neighborhood, etc., PERIOD!

You must accept, without reservations, that you are where you are and you are who you are because of *you*. Your life is the sum total of the decisions you either made or did not make at pivotal points in your life. If you want things to change, you must change first.

Your thoughts determine your life. You are always free to choose the context of your conscious mind, your thoughts. You are always responsible for the consequences of those thoughts. Your thoughts determine your attitude, and your behavior. These determine your success or failure.

You were conditioned from infancy to believe someone or something else is responsible for your life. When you are a child, your parents take care of everything. They provide you with food, clothing, shelter, educational opportunities, money, recreations, medical attention, and whatever else you need.

You are entirely provided for by others. You're not responsible for food; it is provided. You're not responsible for clothes; someone buys them. You're not responsible for your education. You just go where you're told and do what you're told, and it is all provided. It's normal and natural for our parents to provide for us during our formative years—the tragedy is when we step into adulthood with the conscious or unconscious expectation that somewhere, somehow, someone *else* is still responsible.

The failure to accept that you are completely in charge of your own life is the source of your unhappiness and underachievement. The job of your parent is to bring you into the world and raise you to the age of eighteen. These are the years in which your job is to gain the skills needed to live life as a fully functional adult—everything needed to enter maturity as a fully responsible, self-reliant adult capable of making decisions.

Whether or not you were well-prepared is irrelevant from this point forward. From the age of eighteen onward, you are the architect of your own destiny. Whether or not your parents have succeeded in raising you as a totally reliant individual, from that moment onward, there is no looking back. Everything you are, everything you become from then on, is you.

Everyone has a white rabbit—sometimes, many white rabbits. These are the excuses you use to avoid setting clear goals and making total commitments in your life. You need to become a skilled thinker if you desire to fulfill your potential. Part of being a skilled thinker is for you to objectively analyze any mental block or excuse holding you back, any reason for not making progress. Some of the white rabbits people use as excuses are self-limiting ideas. I'm too young, or I'm too old, or I don't have money. I don't have enough education. I have too many bills or I am not ready. I cannot do it because of my boss, my children, my parents, my spouse, or some other reason. Now, what are your white rabbits? What are your favorite excuses for not making the changes you know are necessary to make in order to achieve your goals and fulfill your dreams? You need to go rabbit hunting!

Carefully analyze them to see if they have any validity. Here is a simple test to ask yourself: is there anyone, anywhere with my problem or limitation who has succeeded despite it? If the answer is yes, then you know that your excuse is not legitimate going ahead. Whatever one person does, you can do, too.

There are many single mothers, recovering addicts, ex-cons, people coming out of poverty that have use their struggles as a springboard to success. Refuse to make excuses. Instead, make a conscious decision to thrive. Overcome the past by sculpting a future of your choosing. You can do it. Just cook the rabbits.

The acceptance of complete responsibility and giving up all your excuses is not easy. It is exceedingly difficult, and that is why most people never do it. As an adult you can never give responsibility away. The only thing you can give away is control. If you try to make someone or something else responsible, you are giving up control. However, you still end up being 100 percent responsible and in addition you will feel negative or angry or anxious or depressed. Self-responsibility is a quality of the fully mature, fully functioning, self-actualizing individual. High performers take both the credit and the blame for everything that happens. Low performers only take the credit for successes, and they blame their failures on bad luck or other people or circumstances beyond their control.

Successful individuals have a sense of accountability that extends to their work and relationships. In accounting, the term "balancing the books" means making up for a loss. If an account has a deficit, you balance the books. You must first take all the losses, all the deficits, and total them up. Then you will know your deficit and how much you need to add to balance the book.

When the books become balanced, nobody can tell there was ever a loss. In the same way, you need to balance the books in your life.

We all go through things that put us at a deficit—a rough childhood, the loss of a loved one, something that doesn't make sense, etc. If nothing changed to confront the losses, we would be out of balance. For individuals struggling with addiction or incarceration, being out of balance is perilous. Life is not always fair. You may go through seasons when you are out of balance. You are still responsible for balancing your books.

You must add up the losses, the disappointments, the heartaches. By meticulously and methodically auditing your books, you master the art of balancing and keeping things in order. Failures make other people accountable.

We are all self-employed, irrespective of who signs our paycheck or where we work. You are the president of your own personal services corporation. You are in charge; you are the boss of SELF Inc! Look upon your company as if it belongs to you. This is called intrapreneurship; you get all the experience of running a business without taking on any of the expenses or liability. Consider it a training preparing you for a future-orientated purpose. See yourself as self-employed. Act as if you own the place. When you refer to your company use words like "we" and "our" and "us." Low performers refer to the company as something separate from them. They think it is a job with no other significance. There is a direct relationship between how much responsibility you are willing to accept and how high you will rise.

There is a direct relationship between the following: your income, your status, your position, your prestige, your recognition, and the amount of responsibility you are willing to take on, without excuses, for achieving the company's goals and objectives. You will be compensated accordingly. If you were an employer and you had two people working: one who treated the company as if it belongs to him (intrapreneur), and another who treated it as just a job, a place to be from nine to five, which one would you promote? Which one would you invest in and pay a premium for services?

Your attitude toward self-responsibility is an important statement about the person you are. I think you can put everyone on a scale from high to low acceptance of responsibility.

A highly responsible person tends to be positive, optimistic, self-confident, self-reliant. A person at the other end of the equation with an attitude of irresponsibility will be negative, pessimistic, defeated, unsure, and often neurotic and mentally unstable.

Self-responsible individuals tend to be extremely healthy and positive, mentally. Irresponsible individuals tend to be unhealthy and negative, mentally. There is a direct relationship between how much responsibility you accept in any area of your life and how much control you feel in that area. There is a direct relationship between how much control you feel in any given area and how much freedom you feel you have in that area. Responsibility, control, and a sense of freedom go hand in hand. There is a direct relationship between how much responsibility, how much control, how much freedom, and how many positive emotions you enjoy.

There is a relationship between how much responsibility you accept and how much positive mental attitude you have. At the lower end of the spectrum, a person who feels he is not responsible for his life also feels a lack of control, or out of control entirely.

There is no need for negative emotions. They serve no purpose. They are harmful; they're the reason we fail to grow and evolve to higher levels of consciousness. No one is born with negative emotions. Every negative emotion we experience as adults we learn starting in childhood through a process of imitation, practice, repetition, and reinforcement.

Since all negative emotions are learned, they can be unlearned. We can be free of them. Many people have experienced negative emotions for so long that they find it difficult to accept that they can be eliminated. Whatever you believe with feeling becomes your reality. I love and agree with this Henry Ford quote: "If you think you can or think you cannot, either way you are right." If you absolutely believe negative emotions are necessary in your life, then they certainly will be and will remain so.

Let's look at some of the identifiable negative emotions. There is doubt and fear. There is also guilt and resentment, which tend to go together like twins. There is also envy and jealousy, the great destroyer of happiness and relationships.

There are many negative emotions, but they all eventually are expressed in the form of anger. Anger is the worst of all the negative emotions. Anger is either inwardly expressed—that will make yourself sick—or outwardly expressed, making others sick—especially, making them sick of being around you and your anger.

How do you feel when your angry? You cannot concentrate. You become totally occupied with the object of your anger. You talk furiously. The longer your anger goes the more consuming it becomes, like a fire burning out of control.

It can rob you of sleep, of friends, and of employment. It can cause you to behave irrationally and act in ways that make you feel ashamed or embarrassed. Does anything good ever come out of a negative emotion? Your answer to this question will reveal a scope of where you are and how far you need to go. Negative emotions tied to irresponsibility serve no purpose. Why then do people experience so many negative emotions?

There are four main causes of all negative emotion. The first cause is justification. Justification take place when we justify and explain to ourselves and others why we are entitled to this negative emotion, why we are entitled to feel angry. You can begin the elimination of negative emotions by simply refusing to justify your negative emotions. Refuse to allow yourself the luxury of creating all kinds of reasons why you are entitled to feel angry. You find that all judging of others eventually leads to some form of condemnation and the negative emotions of intolerance and eventually anger go with the condemnation. In the Bible it says, "judge not lest ye be judged." Have you ever driven along in traffic getting cut off by another driver? Do you notice how angry you become? Even though you have never seen the driver before, and the other driver has never seen you, you react as if the driver had carefully plotted your route and waited to ambush you. The moment you stop telling yourself what a terrible driver that person is and just laugh it off, your anger just dissipates and quickly disappears.

The second cause of negative emotion is identification, that is, taking things personally. You can only become angry about something to the degree you can personally identify with the situation and see it as negatively affecting you in some way. The minute you stop taking things personally, the minute you begin to start practicing some form of detachment or what is called dis-identification, standing back from the situation, your negative emotion will begin to diminish. Individuals that remain calm and unemotional longer than the average person refuse to justify or get caught up in the heat of the moment. They refuse to take things personally, instead looking at them from the viewpoint of a detached observer. This control makes them effective in dealing with the crisis.

The third factor of negative emotions is lack of inconsideration. We become angry when we feel people are not giving us our just due. When people are not respecting or recognizing us in the way we feel entitled to, or if someone is rude or doesn't pay enough attention to us in a social situation, we feel angry, hurt, or defensive. You should not worry about what people think of you. If you knew how seldom they did think of you, you would be insulted!

You can begin to eliminate negative emotions by refusing to justify them and refusing to create reasons for them. By refusing to identify with things and take things personally. By refusing to let the behaviors of others get to you.

The fastest way to eliminate is to go right to the cause. The astonishing fact is 99 percent of your negative emotions depend, for existence, on your ability to blame someone or something else for something you do not like. Blaming is the fourth cause of negative emotions. The minute you stop blaming, when you refuse to blame anyone or anything, your negative emotion concedes. The simple switch that you can use to short circuit any negative emotion is the conscious mind.

Remember again, it can hold one thought at a time, positive or negative, and you are the only one who determines which one.

Whenever you feel negative or angry you can immediately cancel out the thought by assertively declaring, "I am responsible." The words "I am responsible" pivot your mindset from negative to positive. It enables you to assert complete control over your emotions converting them into a positive. They cause you to be calm to see the situation with greater clarity. The words "I am responsible" put you in charge, equipping you with the fortitude needed to deal with the situation effectively. Here is the critical factor: you can't develop further in life with your negative emotions intact. The personal growth needed to secure your freedom will require the systematic elimination of negative emotions.

It is not possible for you to excel to a higher level of consciousness except to the degree to which you free yourself from your negative emotions. Free yourself from the forces incarcerating your current reality. This acceptance of responsibility, the elimination of negative emotions, is not optional—it is mandatory! It is essential to your health and happiness and personal development.

The ability to evoke positive thoughts and behaviors at will in your life is characterized in the elimination of negative emotions. It would enable you to start using your higher mental powers. As an exercise of clearing your mind, pause for a moment and meditate on your life. Think and look over your past and present, then systematically analyze the memory or situation that causes you to feel negative. You will quickly learn, if you're totally honest with the self-inventory, how these four elements permeated the outcome in those situations. I would propose you just stop reading and do the exercise before you continue. Develop insight of these experiences to alleviate the barriers holding you back. Make a choice right now. There are some things that must be eliminated immediately. If you really want things to change, go into your personal iceberg and start to reveal more of the real you.

Neutralize the negativity associated with the memory by saying, "I am responsible." The fact of the matter is that you are responsible. Whatever adversity you have as an adult you got yourself into it. You were free to choose. You probably knew at the time you should not be doing it, but you did anyway. You are completely responsible for what happened and the consequences thereafter.

Responsibility looks forward, to the future. Blame looks backward, looks for the person who is going to be punished. If someone runs into your car at a light, you are not at fault, but you are responsible for how you react to the event. You are responsible for your conduct and your behavior. You can either respond by becoming angry and emotional just like a baby when it throws a tantrum, or you can respond by being mature and in control. It's always your choice.

Everything is contained in your response, not the situation. You can't control the event, but you're in control of the response. Many people make adjustments in their lives after learning these principles. There are a few who will declare there is no way they will accept responsibility in this one area of their life. They refuse to let go and instead choose to hold on. They will say, "If you only knew what that person did to me, you would understand." My answer is that the existence of one negative emotion in your conscious or subconscious mind is sabotaging your chances for peak outcomes.

Imagine buying a BMW, beautiful and perfect. There's one problem though—a mistake made assembling one front brake. It is locked on and cannot be released. You depart the dealership with your beautiful new car and anxiously get on the road. Everything in the car is perfect, except that one front wheel brake that is locked on. When you step on the gas to accelerate, the car starts to spin around that locked wheel. The car is going around and around in a circle. No matter how hard you step on the gas or how much you twist the wheel, you simply go around in a circle.

The world is full of people just like that. They may be intelligent, well-educated, and seem to have everything going for them, but their lives just seem to go around in a circle. The reason is that they are holding on to at least one key area where they are refusing to accept responsibility. I know many individuals who are still angry over something that happened to them during their childhood. This refusal to accept responsibility hurts their relationships with their spouses, their children, their co-workers, and their friends. It will manifest itself in a variety of psychosomatic illnesses. We are not wired to carry these burdens.

Here is an exercise for you. Take a sheet of paper and draw a line down the middle vertically. On the left side, make a list of every person or situation for which you harbor negative feelings. On the right side, write a series of sentences that begin with "I am responsible for this because:" and complete this sentence. Do this for each item. Be brutally honest; be as hard on yourself as you could possibly be. Write every reason and answer for why you might be responsible for what happened. When you have completed this exercise, you will feel empowered, free, and in control of your life. You will start to ascend your self-esteem and self-awareness to move you in the direction of peak performance. You are responsible!

7

CHARACTER

There are many virtues, values, and behaviors that go into a person of character. Honesty, generosity, courage, and persistence are fundamental virtues. Every leader should have enough emotional maturity to separate from the pack and go against the grain. You should insist on staying disciplined to yourself, your values, and your goals. You should overcome ridicule, the opinions of others, and criticism meant to destroy or tear down. Whenever you are getting criticized, attacked, or talked about, receive it as affirmation that you are cultivating a path of success.

Here, you will buckle down and stay focused, erecting the resilience only available to a true champion. You will drastically see the people you must eliminate from your circle. Here is a simple rule: if you're the smartest person in your circle, you need to find a new circle. You cannot live in a circle where only you are making emotional deposits. You will become emotional bankrupt. They will drain you with their constant withdrawal of time and energy. You must surround yourself with people that complement your pursuit of your vision, goals, and purpose.

Act like a giraffe, not a turtle. Turtles move slow, they stink, and have limited vision to what's before them. They will get crushed by a giraffe in an instant. Giraffes hold their heads up high and therefore have the luxury of seeing yards ahead with no infringement on their vision. They're just like Peyton Manning, able to see all the receivers, tight ends, and running backs downfield. He knows all his options on any giving play, delivering the ball exactly where he wants.

Keep repeating the words of the Toys R Us commercial with one minor adjustment to the lyrics: "I want to grow up, I do not want to be a kid!" That is emotional intelligence, knowing what must be done. And then, you execute! Emotional maturity means acting like an adult in every situation. Little children throw tantrums, not adults. Adults act mature, are in control of their words, and respond calmly to any situation. They never lose control or throw tantrums. We all have opportunities to be joyful or get upset and go around frustrated. Life is full of inconveniences, delays, and people who do us wrong. You are never going to stop these things from happening; the key is how we handle them. No one can take your joy. That means you control your joy. Nothing can take it from you; you choose to give it away.

Life is too short to live frustrated, upset about things that, many times, we have no control over. People have a right to their opinion, but you have a right to ignore them. People have a right to be rude, but you have a right to stay happy. Quit letting insignificant things—your grouchy boss, the person talking behind your back, someone getting on your nerves—steal your joy. Make this decision every morning: "I will be joyful today." When you are tempted to get upset, remind yourself that you have the power to keep your joy. If you can master this in prison, you will become well-trained in directing your responses to a situation by the time you reintegrate into society.

You can distill all the virtues in the world down into two qualities: integrity and self-discipline. When you become a well-disciplined person of high integrity, you will live your life consistent with the essential virtues, elevating the character of a superior person.

The most important quality that you can develop is the quality of integrity. It is the key to a successful and happy life, and a happy spouse. It is the essential precondition for achievement. Integrity is the core quality of the superior person. Your commitment to becoming totally honest will assure your happiness.

Integrity is a value, like persistence and courage. It is the value that guarantees all the other values. You are a good person to the degree that you live life consistent with the high values you espouse. Integrity is the quality that looks at your values and causes you to live in accordance with them, consistently. A person with integrity is a person of high character. You cannot be a little pregnant. You are either pregnant or not. The same is true with integrity—either you have it, or you don't.

Integrity is the foundation of character development. Let it be one of the activities you engage in for the rest of your life. Working on your character means disciplining yourself to do more of those things a thoroughly honest person does.

To be impeccably honest with others, you must first be impeccably honest with yourself. You must be authentic to yourself. A person living consistently with honorable virtues is living a life of integrity. When you commit to living this kind of life, you will find yourself continually raising your standards, continually redefining the true definition of integrity and honesty for yourself.

You can measure how high your level of integrity is by looking at the things you do and the order in which you do them. You can look at your reactions and responses to the inevitable ups and downs you face. You can observe the things you do and then you will know the kind of person you really are. For example, the external manifestation of high integrity is high quality work. A person who is totally honest with themselves will be someone who does or strives to do excellent work in every situation.

For example, if you need a GED, you put every ounce of effort into the endeavor of getting one. You will be exhibiting a high level of integrity to yourself. Take the same number of hours available for the pursuit of achieving your goal into playing video games and you are lacking high integrity. If you are transitioning from incarceration, you can't be neglecting yourself in these critical areas of growth.

The above examples illuminate how one act of deprivation in one area will become a habit that will compound other areas of your life. The inverse effect is also true—if you focus on high integrity in one area, simultaneously you will grow in another.

The totally honest person recognizes, sometimes unconsciously, that everything they do is a statement about who they are. When you commit to start a little earlier, work a little harder, stay a little later, and concentrate a little more on the important details in your life, you are practicing integrity. You can use these principles in relationships, in being a husband/wife, a father/mother, and even a leader.

The law of attraction says you attract into your life the people and circumstances that are in harmony with your dominant thoughts or values. This means that everything in your life you have attracted to yourself because of the person you are. If there is anything in your life, work, or relationships you are not happy with, you must work on yourself so that you can ultimately receive the desired outcomes.

You are the cause and the effect in every aspect of your existence. Your life only becomes better when you become better. Before you can have more, you must first be more. All of life is lived from the inside out.

At the very core of your personality lie your values about yourself and your life. Your values determine the kind of person you really are. It is what you believe in that defines your character and your personality. It is what you stand for and what you will not stand for that tells you and the world what kind of person you have become.

What are the five most important values in your life right now? My five most important values are God, family, vocation, service, and continuous personal growth and development. Your answer to this question will reveal an enormous amount about you. What would you pay for, sacrifice for, suffer for, or die for? What would you stand up for or refuse to lie down for—what are the values that you hold onto? Think carefully, and when you get a chance, write them down. Here is another way of looking at these questions: what person, living or dead, do you most admire? Once you pick two or three of them, the next questions are: why do you admire them? What values, qualities, or virtues do they have that you respect and look up to? Can you articulate them? What is it that you would most like to emulate?

This is the point of initiating your values. This forms the foundation of your character, the first floor of your high riser. How can you tell what your true values are? Look at the things you do when you're feeling tension. Under duress, you will choose what you most value. What do you do when you are broke, there is no food, and you are not working? What are your thoughts, how do you respond? What's important, and in what order? Is family important, are freedom and being sober important?

All of life will challenge you to make choices. You should continually evaluate how effective these choices are and the impact they have on your life. If your thoughts are not producing the desired results, then you need to make better choices. It is that simple. Nothing more, nothing less.

Whenever you are presented with a choice of how to spend your time, your money, or your emotions, you will elect the choice that is consistent with your highest value. If you make better choices, you will get better results. Your values are expressed in your behavior. It is not what you say that counts; it is what you do. You can tell who a person really is by observing what they do, especially when you need to make a choice between two values.

A person's adherence to values produces opulence in character. Customers rank integrity of a salesperson as the number one quality to determine if they do business. In true leadership, the number one quality is integrity. Integrity in leadership is expressed in terms of truthfulness and consistency. It is manifested in allegiance to keeping your word. Trust is the adhesive holding it all together in all relationships.

Integrity is essential for society. In its absence it would be impossible to conduct the simplest transactions. We could not make a purchase without a level of assurance that the price was correct.

Your personal assets are how you are known. Your personal reputation for keeping your word and fulfilling your commitments are vital. How does your integrity measure with your spouse and your children? Your integrity and your adherence to your values precede you and they affect all your interactions.

Define the three to five most important values in your life. Organize them in order of priority. Then, write a small paragraph defining what they mean to you. A value combined with a definition becomes an organizing principle, a statement for making better choices, a measure enabling you to comprehend your level of adhering to your innermost beliefs and convictions.

For example, if your family is your innermost valuable belief, you might define it something like this: "My family takes precedence over all other things. My family is the most important element in my existence. Whenever I must choose between my family and anything else, including money, possessions, success, or other rewards, I always choose the happiness of my family. Things that are important should never be found on the same road as things that are not important."

Using the above example of family being the most important value and belief, ask yourself if you were totally sincere about the statement that you would never go back to prison. In addition, the values you exemplify to your family will reciprocate back to you accordingly. If family is the most important value and you end up in prison again, then the statement you proclaimed to the world is that the situation you engaged in that took you back to prison was more important than your family. You just have not taken responsibility. The fact that you choose not to adhere to your values will not exempt you from reality.

If you use a defining mission statement for your primary values, you can always access them to guide and discipline you to live congruently with your innermost values and your own definition according to your mission statement. Do what you claim to do. If you just do what you proclaim to do, you will accomplish some great things.

You can revolutionize your character and integrity by studying people of character. Study the lives of people you admire. Study a character whose strength and resilience are empowering. Imagine how they would handle the barriers you're facing.

What would they do?

If you start to produce a feeling, you would act in accordance to the manner of that feeling. If you feel happy, you act happy. If you feel angry, you act angry. If you act the way you would act if you accomplished something important to you, acting will generate the feelings that go with it.

You can, in effect, act your way into feeling an emotion. You can fake it until you make it. You can pretend you have that already, and a reverse effect will cause you to feel what you're pretending to have. If you want to be enthusiastic, act enthusiastic. If you want to be successful, act, think, and feel successful.

In character development, you can become great by acting exactly as you would if you were already the kind of person that you would most like to become. If you believe you are a person of integrity you will create the mental structure and habits of such a person. Your action will become your reality. You will create your personality in harmony with your highest aspirations. The payoff from acting with integrity is that you are very intricately connected to how you feel about yourself.

The more you work, talk, and behave with your highest value the more you will like yourself and the better you will feel. Your self-image improves and your level of self-acceptance goes up. You will respect yourself more.

There are three areas of your life in which you demonstrate your integrity. These are the areas of temptation or the areas of opportunities. When you listen to your inner voice and when you do what you know to be the right thing, you will have a sense of peace that leads to greater outcomes.

The first area of integrity is your relationships with your family and friends, the people closest to you. Being true to yourself means living in truth with each person. Living in truth means refusing to say something you do not feel or believe is right. Living in truth with people means you refuse to stay in any situation where you're unhappy. You refuse to tolerate it; you refuse to compromise, justify, or rationalize.

Stress comes from trying to live in a way not congruent with your highest values. When your life is out of alignment, that is when you feel unhappy. When you are doing and saying one thing on the outside but really feeling something different on the inside, you will feel stress. For individuals who struggle with cycles of incarceration or recovery, living under duress and unhappiness is a guaranteed relapse without the intervention to remove yourself from toxicity.

When you decide to become a person of integrity, your actions will offset all the barriers in relationships. You extinguish the fires in your life. You do that by honestly confronting the individual and divulging the degree of your unhappiness. Be assertive in expressing the desire to reorient the relationship by augmenting prosperity. If the person is reluctant to adjust, be brutally honest with yourself. This should make it clear you do not want to stay in this relationship. Don't let years or decades stop you from doing what's right for you, and don't attempt to buy or win love.

Pouring money into a relationship will leave you bankrupt, monetarily and emotionally. Doing thoughtful acts of kindness will not win you the lottery. In the end, you will lose yourself and the relationship. Save your money and thoughtful kindness for the person who will capture your heart based on the fulfillment of a true partnership. Detach the neurotic person; you are not a lifeguard.

The second area of integrity is your attitude and behavior toward money. A casual attitude toward money brings causalities in your life. You must be fastidious about your treatment of money especially other people's money. You must guard your credit rating the same way you would guard your honor because how you manage it will convey your integrity. You must pay your bills on time, or even sooner! Keep your promises regarding financial commitments.

The third area of integrity is your promises to others. The rule is simple: always keep your word. Be a person of honor. If you say you will do something, do it. If you make a promise, keep it. If you make a commitment, fulfill it. Be known as the person who someone else can trust no matter what. Integrity is key in character. Your integrity forms the foundation of your life. Practice integrity like you practice breathing.

Character is the ability to follow through after the emotion in which the resolution was made is dispersed. Your character is manifested in your willingness to adhere to the values you hold. It is easy to make promises and not keep them but, if you keep your promise, it will make your character stronger. As you improve every part of your life will improve. There is a quality of self-discipline that goes with integrity and will guarantee greater outcomes.

Self-discipline will solidify your accomplishments in whatever you aspire toward. Self-discipline is important. If you don't develop it to a monumental horizon, it will be a challenge to achieve what you're capable of achieving. Self-discipline is a habit and a lifestyle.

When you develop the levels of high personal discipline possessed by successful people, you begin to achieve the same results. Success begets success! Success is preceded by sustained periods of focused effort with determination to arrive at your chosen destination. Here's an acronym to secure your FOCUS: Follow One Course Until Successful.

To achieve anything perpetual you must endure long and often unappreciated hours, months, and years of robust discipline. You must pay this sacrifice in advance. There are no shortcuts. You cover the cost in the moment, accelerating your daily deposits.

Self-discipline is something you can learn by continuous practice.

Once you master delayed gratification—the ability to discipline yourself, to keep your attention on the task in front of you—there's no goal you cannot accomplish.

The words "almost done" means you will not finish. Successful people are those who ration their time on high value tasks. Unsuccessful individuals are those who waste minutes on low-value activities. There is a crowding-out principle in time management; this principle says that if you engage in highly productive activities, at the end of the day, you lack sufficient time for unproductive tasks.

If you spend time on low-value activities, those that you inadvertently abridge the time at your disposal to complete what can make all the difference in your life. The key that separates you from both these outcomes rests in your ability to be disciplined with the important matters in life. Below are six disciplines you need to develop.

The first is the discipline of goals. This means that you sit with a pad of paper, a pen, and ample time. You think through the written list of all you want to accomplish in the next year. You organize the list into various areas of your life, career, money, family, health, and any other part of your life that's important. Set priorities among your goals, rewriting your goals in order of importance. Take out a separate piece of paper and write down a list of the things you can work on now in the attainment of your goals.

About 97 percent of adults are trying to live their lives without clear, specific, and written goals. This is the same as setting off on a trip driving to California from New York without a roadmap. You may get somewhere eventually, but it will take you much longer and it is more likely you will get lost and waste an enormous amount of time.

If you plan your trip with a roadmap preparing for the future terrain, the arrival is advanced and damage from the turbulence is minimized. This is what setting goals accomplishes. You will not breakdown on the road, run out of gas, get off the wrong exit, or get a flat tire.

The second discipline is planning. People think they're too busy to plan, but you save ten minutes in execution for every minute you plan. Taking time to contemplate how you will utilize the days ahead is not complicated. Incorporate a planner, using it on a regular basis. Another way of saying this: you work it until you master it. You make a list of the things you want to accomplish, and then you will accomplish them.

If you desire to earn $75,000 a year, how much does it break down to on a monthly and weekly basis? How does it breakdown into cash earned per day and per hour? Once you determine how much you need to make every hour, you can methodically arrange every hour, engaging in the behaviors and outcomes needed to yield your desired hourly wage.

You never compromise to accept minimum-wage activities if you aspire to earn $50 an hour. All your actions for achieving that wage should be in the $50 realm. If you need to improve with education to get you there, then you should not consume hours of playing video games. That is the equivalent of having the potential to earn $50 an hour which is then rejected to earn minimum wage. To earn $50 an hour means denying minimum-wage activities.

You discipline yourself adamantly by prohibiting anything that pays less than the dollar amount you have predetermined. Do you think, if you sat down to chill in the park, someone would approach you with an offer to pay the dollar amount you are seeking?

This is the tradeoff. Surrender to those things that only pay your desired rate. You will discipline yourself to reserve the hours in your day for only working on things that bring you closer to achieving the goal.

The third discipline is budgeting. This applies to your time and money. Individuals accomplishing exuberant outcomes give an enormous amount of thought to the use of their time and money. Give immense thought to how you budget these resources. Institute a planner and know exactly where you will be, with whom, and for how long you are going to be there.

When you speak to individuals who don't harness a planner, you will see that they can't forecast what they'll be doing next Thursday. They have no idea. These individuals assume life is arbitrary. Every stop sign is a new undertaking. They find a crossroad with no concept insofar as which direction to go. The days become disoriented, lacking an entry to the pathway of securing valuable outcomes.

When you plan your time, do so in fifteen-minute blocks so that you know exactly where you should be, who you will be with, and what you will be doing. It is virtually impossible to end up with the wrong person, in the wrong place, at the wrong time if you incorporate this strategy. It is totally impossible to go back to prison or relapse when you are adamantly planning your day. You will find the time to do only the things of higher outcomes. You accomplish more, you get compensated more. The act of budgeting time and money causes you to use both effectively.

The fourth discipline is self-respect. This is observing yourself as the auditor of your life. This is seeing yourself as self-employed. You see yourself as the president of Self Inc. You are creating branding and advertisements for your esoteric gifts. In the world of business, that acumen equates to more worth and, therefore, more money.

The more important you establish yourself to be to an employer, the more income you will generate for your services. You will become irreplaceable. You will create a position for life as an intrapreneur. You will run the company like is yours—without the overhead, expenses, and liability. This is the ultimate training program for you to inevitably become an entrepreneur, if you desire.

The habit of seeing self as an independent contractor and selling your services is a powerful paradigm shift. You will pivot into the journey of optimal and proficient income.

Remember, you are always competing, so step up or get left behind. We don't have the luxury to rest. We rested enough in our years of incarceration. We shouldn't be concerned about leisure. It's time to get to work, my people. We need to continuously strive to separate ourselves from those with both more experience and education who are salivating for the same opportunities available to us.

The fifth discipline is result orientation. This is the attribute of high performance with its equivalent of being paid highly. Results-oriented people think continuously in terms of outcomes. They acknowledge themselves as highly productive people with responsibilities and never lose sight of the important things that need to be executed.

What's the best value of your time right now? What can you do well to advance your life and income? If you could only do one task, what does it look like? Your ability to concentrate on one important thing, remaining true to its attainment, determines your outcomes. The inverse is the reason for failure.

The sixth discipline is action orientation. This requires you to develop excellency in taking action rigorously in relation to the important task. Once you engulf yourself in it, you stay with it till it is completed. Create the fast tempo pathway to do only the things deemed necessary. I repeat: do it now! When you identify that something needs to be taken care of, get it done immediately. Don't procrastinate; earn the reputation for doing the job quickly. When you can combine your thoughts and set specific priorities, you can establish the tools needed to move you forward.

Discipline weighs ounces, but regrets weigh tons! Success is tons of discipline. Self-discipline is the ability to make yourself do what you should do, when you should do it, whether you feel like it or not. Become the person who implements the habits of doing what unsuccessful people don't like to do. What are those things? The same things successful people don't like to do, either. But successful people do them anyway. They do them first with the understanding that doing so is the price of success.

Plan your work and work your plan. Take time to think through responsibilities before you begin. Make unambiguous, unequivocal choices, then implement them quickly. Master getting more done in a shorter period. Focus and be disciplined. The most important benefit of self-discipline is the personal benefit that you receive.

Every act of self-discipline stimulates your self-esteem. It gives you a feeling of power and accomplishment. As you discipline yourself to persist in the face of distractions, diversions, and disappointments, you will feel vibrant in your victories.

Discipline yourself to achieve more and be more. As you achieve, you will start to feel like a winner. Your self-confidence goes up, and you will feel joyful in getting more done. You will earn the respect and esteem of people around you and make more money.

The more things you do, the more things you achieve, employing personal habits of effectiveness and productivity. Your life starts to shape in an upward spiral of success and happiness. You will feel great most of the time! Every act of self-discipline strengthens every other discipline in your life. Every time you do something that weakens you, it weakens your other disciplines as well. When you make a habit of disciplining yourself in little things, it automatically sets you up to achieve bigger things.

Your entire life is an ongoing battle between doing what is right and necessary and doing what is fun and easy. It is a battle between the forces of discipline and the forces of expediency.

When I started my transformation, I was always invited to attend frivolous activities, producing no authentic value in the pursuit of growth. There was always something—festivals, special events, movies, sports. My training with these encounters equipped me to avoid the same minefields in a free society. You are asked to go out for drinks even though they know your history with alcohol. Remember: relapse always leads to prison. I do not play lotto, so why would I gamble with my life? They want your time in activities that are not in harmony with the pursuit of a greater self and greater outcomes— those activities take you back to prison.

When you develop the character that gives you complete self-mastery, self-control, and self-discipline, you will start to feel good about yourself. You will develop an inner strength. You will replace positive thinking with positive knowledge. You will eventually reach the point within where you absolutely know that you could do whatever it takes for yourself.

Self-discipline pays off in terms of a greater self-esteem and a positive mental attitude. It pays off throughout your life in terms of the goals you achieve and the success you attain. Self-discipline is a skill and a habit that can be learned with practice. Each time you practice a little self-discipline you will become stronger to resist the forces detracting you from your mission, purpose, and destiny. You will become greater at managing more disciplines. You will become totally disciplined about your future. The twin qualities of integrity and self-discipline are the foundational qualities of character. Each of these qualities reinforces the other. You will practice integrity by practicing what it is you believe in and stand for.

You will refuse to compromise on your values for anyone or any reason, and you will use your self-discipline to keep yourself on track. Master your emotions and resist temptation to compromise in any part of your life. The more you practice integrity and self-discipline, the better person you will become. As you develop a reputation for integrity and self-discipline, all sorts of doors will open. People will respect you at a higher level. Everything becomes possible for you and your future becomes unlimited. It starts to shape the beginning of an incredible, meaningful, and fulfilling life.

Repeat these principles until they are mastered. Let them become a part of your character and your personality. This will put you on the high road, which is called and defined, by you, as *your life*. You don't get to choose how you're going to die, but you can decide how you are going to live. So why not live it out as a winner, epic in every proportion? Dream big, my brothers and sisters!

8

GOAL SETTING

Only *3 percent* of the people in the world have clear, concise and written goals. The other *97 percent* have vague goals, or no goals. The 3 percent who have clear, written goals earn more than people without goals, even though they both started out at the same starting line and have the same abilities and opportunities. This is especially true with individuals transitioning from incarcerated experiences. Your ability to set goals and make plans for their accomplishment is one of the skills of success. Learn how to master this skill using a principal called idealization.

Let us start with an illustration of the *3 percent vs. 97 percent.*

X X X X X X X X X X X X X X X X X X X X X X X X X X X X X X X X X X X X X X X X X X X X X X X X X X X X X X X X X X X X X X X X X X X X X X X X X X X X X X X X X X X X X X X X X X X X X X X X X X X	X X X
BUS #1	**BUS #2**

Imagine yourself at a bus stop, seeing the arrival of these two buses.

Each X is a representation of each passenger on the bus. Here is a question for you: which bus would you board? Hopefully, you pick bus number two! Bus number two is the path of least resistance. You have all the room you need to operate, travel, and be at peace with little or no distractions. You are in an ideal situation to focus and relax your mind. Bus number one will not provide that for you.

Bus number one barely has room for you. You are amid people anchored by different values and ideologies. Indubitably, you must be attentive and vigilant. In doing so, your focus, energy, and level of stress are exponential. You are subjective to all kinds of attitudes, purviews, bad breath, stinking smells from a lack of a bath, and so many more possibilities of annoyance. You will have to contest every square inch of space. Why would anyone voluntarily subject themselves to that insanity?

Again, I have worked with hundreds of individuals transitioning from incarcerated experiences, accumulating data for every service provided when they get home. The numbers do not lie! If the numbers do not lie, then they must divulge an accurate assessment of the outcomes. If it looks like a duck, walks like a duck, and acts like a duck, it is a freaking *duck!*

WITO Inc. was phenomenal at sequestering individuals away from bus number one. We get them set up with housing, jobs, education, mental health services, and substance abuse prevention services. We advocated for them with parole, got them mentorship in finance, budget, and credit, facilitated life skills workshop, fostered leadership development…the list goes on and on.

Whatever an individual would proclaim to be the essentials for a successful transition, would we find it. I honestly cannot think of one instance where the barriers and challenges were not eradicated for those who developed an honest release plan.

All kind of successes were triumphantly celebrated. Many would go on to enjoy years of living right. One would assume they have finally left the stinking number one bus forever. Many, however, even after much success, retreated to their original destination and voluntarily boarded bus number one all over again. For some, this is where they felt more comfortable—and this is real talk, I am not making it up!

Being responsible for someone who has never been responsible to begin with can freak people out. Those who have been in prison understand this in the form of having someone set a structure for you. They prefer being told when to take a shower, when to eat, and when to go to work. They say it is so much easier than real life challenges—for example, paying bills, the demands of a job, the daily rat-race mentality, and commuting (especially in New York City, it does not matter what form of transportation you take—it is going to be stressful). One must accomplish all of that in one day, and then you must get up the next morning to do it all over again—and you must do it drug-free. No numbing the stress or the pain. You must deal with the raw emotions. I painted this picture to illuminate how much you will need to focus, plan, and execute to maintain freedom, forever!

Setting goals is the equivalent value of bus number two. There are no traffic jams to the road of success. It literally leaves tracks for you to follow. Do what they do and, to that degree, you will also be successful. If you master setting goals, you are on your way toward successful outcomes.

You will be allowed to travel on the path with the least resistance. You will operate your vision and purpose to freedom and the peace that derives from controlling your own destiny. You will eliminate all distractions and genuinely focus on the things you want by defining that personal desire of success you aspire toward.

A person with goals makes progress even on the roughest road. A person without goals goes back and forth even though the road is smooth and clear. A person with goals is like a ship using a compass, a map, a rudder, and a skilled person at the helm. They can sail straight and true to the destination of his/her choosing. A person without goals is like a ship without a rudder, without a compass or maps. They are simply rocking back and forth with the tides, making no progress even in the calmest sea.

To achieve all that you can achieve, you must develop a clear sense of direction. You must decide what you want in every area of your life. The men and women who went back to bus number one and ultimately back to prison decided not to answer the question, "what do I really want for my life when I get home?" They answered some of the questions but obviously felt the barriers between them and a successful life would not pose a challenge—or, they were arrogant, resistant to change in the area that led to their destruction. What do you really want to do with your life? Most people are too confused to define this question. Therefore, they fall short of reaching their potential.

Here is an example: many individuals, when asked what they want to do with their life, will answer, "I want to go to college." Simply stating you want to go to college is not enough to answer the question. You are not being specific; your goal is missing too many components to be measurable and attainable.

A good answer would be something like, "I want to enroll in John Jay College and obtain my bachelor's degree in criminal justice by June 2029." This answer has diligence; the speaker's thought process was focused, and they clearly know how to achieve their goal.

I can assure you, I diligently found the answers to my question that could compromise my freedom. I played the scenes in my head over and over. When I was confronted with some of these challenges, I was ready because I practiced prior to my release. Yet, I still encountered situations that paralyzed me. Without proper preparation, these situations could have jeopardized my pursuit of freedom. I simply applied the traits at my disposal as I have in everything else. I was able to press forward to arrive at my dreams.

The ultimate objective in answering the question is to be happy, however you define this! Everything we do is to achieve our happiness in some way. Happiness is a common denominator of successful people staying out of prison. You are only successful to the degree that you can achieve your own happiness.

If you achieve everything in life—money, home, fame, success—but don't achieve happiness, to that degree, you have failed! A good measure of how you are doing in life is to ask yourself what percentage of the time you feel happy. The answer to this question will tell you how far you have come and how far you still need to go.

There are four ingredients of happiness that are common to every person.

The first is your health. Put your health before all other considerations. If you have health, you have everything, but if you lose your health for any reason, to that degree, you are failing. There is not much a person will do or will want to do when feeling sick.

The second is loving relationships. The more people you have in life who love and respect you, the healthier and happier you are.

The third is meaningful work—work that makes a difference and you do well. We are put on earth to be useful in some way. We are only happy when we feel, deep inside, that what we are and do is somehow helping others in a positive way. Upon your release, dedicate your life to doing something uplifting and enhancing the lives of other people. The criminal mentality and the mentality of addiction tells us to take everything we can get. We have to abolishe that!

Those mindsets do not foster a spirit of giving. I can honestly say that the biggest moments of fulfillment in my life have come from the principle of giving. There is no monetary value, relationship, or drug that compensate my soul except when I am genuinely giving of myself. You must experience this to understand, but when you do, you will be changed forever.

The fourth is financial freedom, financial independence. We live in a material world; food, clothing, shelter, transportation, all must be paid for in some way. We are only happy when we have enough money so that we do not have to worry about these critical needs.

When you have high levels of health and energy, good relationships, meaningful work, and financial independence, you will be happy. We're going to illuminate how you can achieve more by deciding exactly what it is you want and then working toward it.

You need a variety of goals to be happy and have balance in your life. Specifically, you need goals in seven areas: personal, family, financial, career, health, social, and spiritual. Each of these goals should fit like a piece of pie in a pie pan—perfectly rounded.

There are always two types of goals: tangible and intangible. Tangible goals are things that you buy or built. For your family these can include a house, a boat, a car, vacation trip, clothes, and toys. Everyone has tangible goals they acquire for their families.

Intangible goals are qualitative goals. These are things that require time, caring, consideration and emotions. They cannot be bought with money. They are indispensable in a healthy family life. These are the benefits your family wants more of. Men and women get caught up in their work, spending hours overtime, leaving early, working late, and working on weekends. We convince ourselves we're doing it for family. But if you ask their families, they prefer people to work less and spend more time at home.

They want more time doing things together, building memories, and sharing golden moments—dance recitals, baseball games, going to the park, going to the beach. This goes back to the discussion of prioritizing your values. If your family is the most important thing in your life, work can never come at the expense of establishing quality family moments. If it ever becomes out of balance, there is no way you will be happy. You will inaugurate pure stress for sure.

Achieving a balance between intangible and tangible goals for your family is essential. Organize and reorganize your life so that you spend time with the people you care about. Make up a dream list with your spouse and child. Play a game call Let's Pretend and ask them to tell you everything they would love to have included in family life. What would they like more of, what would they like less of? What would they like you to stop doing, or would like you to start doing? Ask them if there is anything they would like for you to change. The feedback will provide you with enough data to generate a family mission statement.

Going forward, you do everything in your power to manage and adhere to the request, periodically analyzing if reconstruction is necessary. As things change, so does the family mission statement.

Ideally, you would incorporate the cultivation of the mission statement with all the members of your family. Your family should be thought of as your most important customer because really, they are! You are dependent upon them, and they are dependent upon you for your health, happiness, and wellbeing. You must find the time to be clear about what it is they want and what it is they need from you. Then, you must adapt to those demands in the same way you would respond to your primary and best customer. Remember, your family is your best customer!

The next area is your financial goals. Since you become what you think about, the more you clearly think about your financial life and your financial goals, the better financial life you will have. All of goal setting involves determining where you are now and where it is you want to end up in the future. The planning process requires you to figure out how you are going to get from where you are to where you want to go. It is that simple! Remember the earlier example of defining how much you are worth today. If you sold everything today, that's your net worth.

If you had to sell everything today how much would you get? Is it sufficient? Probably not. This is exactly why your utmost attention and planning are pivotal. You will start to find the solutions that will take you where you need to go for financial sustainability. An asset is something that puts money in your pocket. A liability is something that takes money from your pocket. Robert Kiyosaki, famously known for writing *Rich Dad Poor Dad* and ensuing books on financial literacy, discusses a phenomenal, unique concept. If you own a house and you are making monthly payments to pay down the mortgage, is the house an asset or a liability?

Based on the definitions for an "asset" and a "liability," the one that is accumulating money into their pockets is the bank, so that is an asset for the bank. For the one making the payment, the one whose money is being extracted from their pockets, it is a liability. The school system and society will lead you to believe if you own a house and are making payments you have an asset. The bank will tell you that, the real estate broker will tell you that, when you file your taxes, you enter your figures as an asset—but that is *BOGUS*! I implore you, please read my next book and build up your financial awareness. Get the rules of investments so you can make money!

Determine how much you will need to earn on a yearly, monthly, weekly, daily, and hourly basis. Then determine what you want to earn next year, and the year after that. How much do you want to be earning in five years? Ten years? When do you want to retire and what type of income do you need to retire? The difference between what you have today and what you will need to retire will tell you exactly how much you will need to work on. It will also tell you how much you need to save and invest to retire at your projected time.

How much should you relax and rest, in the most affluent country in the world? Today's retiree has an annual retirement income of $31,000. Is this amount sufficient for you to end your lifetime? If you divide $31,000 by 12 months, you get $2,583.33 a month. Divide that amount by 4.33 to compensate the months with only four weeks and you get $596.61 a week to live out your life for one year. When you get home, you will find many seniors working because they didn't prepare enough for retirement. Individuals who were incarcerated for years or decades will typically find themselves in the same exact situation as the seniors describe above. Does this speak to the degree of preparation to abdicate these barriers? You can overcome it, but it will require the absolute best in you.

Financially successful people are thoughtful and prudent regarding their financial life. They are never broke; they enjoy a higher standard of living even though their incomes are not drastically different than the average person. You see, many of us are utilizing our future dollars for today's lifestyle. This is especially true with credit card debt. You have a choice of making interest payments to a credit card or to yourself in the form a retirement investment. A retirement investment account will pay you interest. One creates an asset, the other shapes a liability.

People are under the assumption that you need an exuberant amount of money to join the financial elite. The reality is you enter this exclusive space by thinking and acting as they do. By actively and consciously accumulating pennies, you inadvertently convert them into dollars and dollars become hundreds with time. That is why is so imperative to start now. Capture as much time as you can while it is readily available. The time to start investing in your future is now!

The second most important choice you make, after marriage, is your career. It is essential you do something you enjoy for which you already have a natural talent. The greatest time-waster is spending years of your life at a job you are unhappy with. This is one of the largest reasons for frustration, addiction, and problems in relationships. Ultimately, it leads to failure in life. So many people work at a job for ten, fifteen, or twenty years complaining. They do not work on improving their skill set, they do not pursue education or training— they just complain about the people they work with, the supervisors, the systems, the rules. In fact, they do not have a resume ready to pursue greater opportunities with the experiences they do have. How can you tolerate this pain of wasted years in your prime and accept it without looking for ways to remove yourself from the toxicity that evolves in the situation?

The great advantage for individuals transitioning is to understand that this is your competition. Any advancement of planning gives you an advantage. Here is a prime example of the ninety-seven vs. three mentality: you become their supervisors or managers if you come home with the belief you are going to thrive. That sounds like money to me.

What are the things that really bring you joy, and that you love to do? What do you enjoy doing that is fun? After self-analyzing all that you now know, would you start at your current job? If your answer is no, the next question is: how do you get out, and how quickly can you do so? The way you can tell if you're in the right job is if you really enjoy it. You do it for free. You strive to be good at it. You get so good at it you get paid well to do it. You are eagerly anxious to learn more and, if need be, you are taking courses to improve in your field. You admire the people in your field. You think about your work constantly and cannot wait to get back when you are off or on vacation. If none of these conditions exist in your work, it is time to give your future career some serious contemplation. It may be the most important thing you do.

Your educational goals are extremely important. Lifetime learning is the minimum requirement for success. If you want to be the best, establish a lifelong learning plan. Be committed to getting better in the important things you do. Education is not only found in college. You may ascertain it via Google, YouTube, reading books, or even volunteering. Get creative and open yourself up to the many possibilities that are out there. If you go to a construction site, you could guess how tall the building would be by how deeply built the foundation is. A tall building would have a foundation of concrete that goes down many floors into the ground. Imagine building a twenty-floor building with rental apartments.

You cannot go back into the foundation, so you can build the building higher. Once the foundation is set it cannot be changed. The height is fixed forever. We are very much like a building. The height to which you can grow is determined by your foundation of knowledge. You do have one great advantage. At any given time, you can go to work and build your foundation deeper. You can add to your house of knowledge. You can build your life higher. The deeper you build your foundation to continue learning, the higher your level of achievement—and there are no limits.

What are your plans to develop the knowledge and skills you need for the future? The competition is fierce! People are gaining on you all the time. Everyone wants to get to the head of the line and enjoy the good life. If you are not getting better, you are getting worse. No one stays in the same place; technology is growing exponentially. If you want to get ahead, you must run, baby. If we slow down, our place will be taken by those more ambitious.

The next set of goals is our health. The average life span is between seventy-six and eighty years old. This means that some people will die before then. It is not hard to see who will pull down the averages—what we eat, how we stress, how we rest, whether (and how) we work out, and whether or not we abuse our bodies with chemicals determines the quality of our lives as we depart from our loved ones. Intelligence is a factor in success, but as the intelligence factor is measured, it illuminates how some people with average intelligence did well while some people with exceptional intelligence did not. What was the difference? The experts conclude that intelligence is not a matter of IQ or academic scores. Intelligence is a way of acting. If you act intelligently, you are smart. If you act stupid, you are stupid. The question then, is: what is an intelligent way of acting?

You are acting intelligently when what you do is moving you toward a goal that is important to you. You are acting stupid when what you are doing is moving you away from the determined goal. Imagine being offered an opportunity to double your income if you obtain a certification in your field. If you took immediate action to secure the certification, you are acting intelligently. If you instead utilized your free time from work to play video games and watch TV, you are acting stupid. These are the people pointing fingers at other people and circumstances in their workplace.

To be an intelligent person, all you need to do is determine exactly what it is you want and then only do things that move you in that direction. Refuse to do anything that doesn't help you achieve the goal. To every request for your time that doesn't move you toward your goal, just say no! What is most important to you? What do you value more than anything else? All stress rises when you depart from your virtues and values. Our emotional and mental problems can be resolved by returning to our values. What would you do, how would you change your life if you won one million dollars? How would you change your life if you had that kind of money at your disposal? What would be the first thing you would do? What would be the second thing, what would you get into or get out of? What would you buy or what financial situation would you resolve?

What is the purpose of this question?

To help you determine what you would do if you had all the time and money you needed. What would you do if you were free to choose your course of action? What would you do if you could do anything you wanted? The reality is, the money is available. So is the time needed. All you must do is decide to do it! Just ask Mike, the famous marketing strategy for Michael Jordan's Nike commercials.

Here is another question: What would you do if, today, you learned you had six months to live? Imagine you are going to enjoy good health for 180 days, and then drop dead! How would you change your life? Who would you want to spend your time with? What would suddenly be important? What would not be important? You would figure out instantly, what's important, and who's important. You would embark on the path you've been avoiding.

This is a value question. This question forces you to ask and answer what is profoundly important to you. When you have a short time to live, all the unimportant things drop away and you are face to face with the things you really care about. Any kind of mental, emotional, or physical imprisonment must be viewed as if your life and time with the important people in your life are limited. Limited, in the sense that at some point in the future you will run out of time to make it happen for you. If you do not change, you will die—metaphorically or literally!

What have you always wanted to do, but been afraid to? Many

people spend their lives with their feet on the brakes, holding back what they really want to do because of fears of some kind. They're afraid they might lose their time or lose their money or lose their emotions. They're afraid others may disappoint or criticize them or make them feel ridiculous. Don't refrain from doing something because you're afraid what people might think. The truth is nobody is really thinking about you at all. Nobody really cares about your life as you do. Most of the people are too consumed by their own problems and their own life. They do not have time to be thinking about you. Whatever you do or not, make your decision based on what you want to do.

What sorts of activities give you the greatest feeling of importance? What lifts your self-esteem, self-respect, and personal pride? What are the activities throughout your life that have made you feel the happiest and most fulfilled? These answers will lead you to your heart's desire. These are the things you have been placed on Earth to do. You could tell what it is by the way it makes you feel when you're doing it. Whatever it is, whatever would give you joy, whatever you wanted to do but been afraid to do, whatever you would do if you won one million dollars, is probably what you were born to do. Each of us are born to do that one thing—it is your responsibility to find out what it is and then throw your whole heart into doing it well!

Now the question becomes: what one thing would you would dare to dream if you knew you could not fail? If you were guaranteed success in any one goal, small or large, short term or long term, what would it be? What one thing would you dare to dream if you knew absolutely you could not fail? Your life begins to become great when you decide on your major definitive purpose and begin to work on it. Goal-setting is, for you, designed to help you reach the point where you can select the most important steps for the planning and attainment of your goals.

Here are seven steps of a goal setting exercise that will propel you to set and achieve goals.

Step 1: Decide what you want and write it down. This activity alone moves you ahead to change the direction of your life. Remember, do not just say "I want to go to college;" be specific. Do not say "I want to make more money." Instead, say "I will increase my hourly wage to $50 by December 31, 2030." Then, you devise the plan and the steps to achieve it.

Step 2: Set a deadline for your goal. Set sub-deadlines, if necessary. Be specific about what you intend to accomplish.

The more specific you are about your deadlines and your dates, the sooner success will arrive. A goal without a date has no urgency; it lacks action, it is just a freaking dream. It's like having a gun without bullets. It is a dummy, a blank.

Step 3: Determine the obstacles you have to overcome to achieve the goal. What are the choke points that determine the speed? What prevents the achievement of your goal? Why aren't you at your goal already? Of all the obstacles you will have to overcome, what are the largest obstacles, the boulders on the path to the goal? What are the pebbles, the easiest? Whatever the challenges are, begin with the one you're most comfortable starting with. For some people, starting with the biggest grants free and easy access the rest of the way. For others, working your way up from the smallest to the biggest gives you the path of least resistance. In either case, you're right, based on your specifics. Start there.

Step 4: Determine the knowledge, skill, and abilities you will need to reach your goals. To achieve something you never achieved before, you must become someone you have never been before. You must develop knowledge and skills you do not have today. Every goal requires that you become a new person in some way.

Step 5: Determine the people, groups, and organizations whose help you will require to achieve your goal. Big goals require the collaboration of lots of people. What will I have to do to earn their support? What will I have to do to earn their backing? Everything comes back to relationships; do not be afraid to ask for help.

Even if it is in the form of advice or introduction from the people you know. One person, one contact, can make all the difference between success and failure. When I got home, I asked for a lot of help—guess what happened? I got a lot of help, which I needed to expedite my pursuit of a new, healthy, and happy me.

I would not have accomplished what I have done today without the help of hundreds. Some big, some small—their contributions helped me find my way, my vision, my purpose.

Step 6: Develop a plan to achieve your goal. Make a list of the obstacles you will have to overcome in the attainment of the additional skills or knowledge you would have to acquire and the people whose help you will need. Organize the list into a plan based on priorities and sequence.

Step 7: This is the most important step. Act immediately on your plan. Once you start, never stop. Do something every day that moves you toward the achievement of your goal. Become intensely action-orientated. Develop a preference for action and a sense for urgency. Be a moving target. Develop the momentum principle. This principle says once you're in motion, it is easier to stay in motion. If you came to a complete halt and try to start again, it will be more exasperating, mentally. Some never get back in motion. Are you willing to take this chance?

Write your goals in the present tense as if you already have achieved them. Write a list of ten goals and, when you are finished, review the list to see which one you want to designate as your number one goal. This goal, if you achieve it, will have the greatest impact on your life. This goal, then, becomes your organizing principle for the next twelve months. It becomes your major, definitive purpose.

Your job is to talk about your goals all day long. Whenever you are worried, think about your goals. Whenever you have a problem, think about your goals. When you wake up, think about your goals. By the law of concentration, whatever you dwell upon grows and increases in your life. Think about what you want, keep your mind off what you do not want, and think about your goals!

You will learn some of the things that have been neglected were readily available to you, always. You will undoubtedly find your definitive, number one goal. When you write your goals anew, you will find they will gradually begin to change from your original goals. You will know what to keep and what to eliminate.

Something amazing begins to take shape between the head and the hand. Goals that you have never thought of before will suddenly appear. To accelerate the process of goal attainment, create a clear mental picture. What would your life look like if you have already achieved your goal?

Each time you write your goal, take a second to play this picture on the screen of your mind. Visualize and imagine your goal as a reality. Imagine the feeling of pride and satisfaction you would feel if the goal has already been accomplished.

The combination of writing and rewriting your goals plus visualizing your goal as a reality mix with the emotions of pleasure and satisfaction you will enjoy. This will have a dramatic effect.

In goal setting, your main job is to be clear about what it is you want. Develop the plan to achieve that goal and then think about it, all the time. Begin working on it every single day. Immediately, you will become a more focused and determined person.

You will become positive, optimistic, and creative. You will begin to activate all the mental powers of your mind and organize all the mental laws to work on your behalf. You will step on the accelerator of your own potential, and you will begin achieving at a higher level. There are no limits except the limits you place on your own imagination.

9

TIME MANAGEMENT

Your ability to manage time and submerge into the assessment of delegating its proper positioning on the things you should be working on now will determine your accomplishments. Success begets success. Replicate the principles many have left behind and duplicate the process. It doesn't matter what you're striving for; do the things successful people do to get the same results. Become well organized. Master the art of organizing time to serve your goals and purpose. Learn to be more productive in less time than the typical person, making you more effective and efficient. Work on only those things that matter and, with time, this will alter your life as you have visualized it. Do it often, do it the right way. Be consistently looking to improve your discernment of your time.

A minimum effort to implement time management principles into your life will harvest an abundancy in your garden of productivity. Step on the accelerator, navigating the outcomes you strive for.

We were introduced to how to work proficiently during our school years with the responsibility of submitting our assignments in a timely manner. The inability to conform then usually continues to be expressed in adulthood when we enter the workforce. According to New York University Business School, 50 percent of adults experienced difficulty focusing and performing a full day at work. I like to draw attention to individuals transitioning. Your life and your freedom are totally dependent on your ability to work a full day with everything you have. You will undermine and sabotage your freedom if you show up with no work ethic. Please tell me you will work harder than you did for any correctional officer who compensated you with donuts or a newspaper. Please tell me you are worth more and you aspire for more.

Individuals who struggled during those academic years developed an incompetency for undertaking responsibilities. Unless the behavior and thinking are renounced this will paralyze their concept of time. They will be continuously abstracted. Engaging on the phone, social media, arriving late, going home early, taking long breaks, are a few samples of their definition of time. It's puzzling when they ask why they haven't received a raise. Do an excellent job and you will be compensated accordingly. There are no barriers to advancement. Because there's a deficiency in the job market, if you show up to do great work, the doors of opportunity are in your reach. You will be hired anytime and anywhere, paid well, and promoted, because there's a shortage of efficient workers.

You can impose the projection to meet the standards in today's job market and excel your potential for an optimal income. Make the decision that you will become proficient at managing your time. Time is your most exquisite possession. If you have an enormous amount of time, you can pursue anything. If time is diminished to any extent your potential is constrained as well.

Anyone on their death bed would take a moment to proclaim; "I would love more time to finish _____." Fill in the blank while you can. Many will not have this opportunity, but you do! The time to appreciate how essential time is will be determined by you and only you! Don't wait to acknowledge this principle until your minutes and hours are dissolving.

There are three rules of time: The first is time cannot be preserved.

This means it can't be saved. It can only be spent. Since time can't be preserved the only alternative is to invest it prudently. You can only modify time from inconsequential activities into substantially productive activities.

When you deposit your time into either activity, you've cashed out and there are no refunds—it is gone forever!

The second rule is time cannot be substituted. There is no back-up plan for time. It doesn't matter what you anticipate doing—watching TV, going for a walk, reading a book—it requires time. Take deliberate time in advance to scrutinize the distribution of your available time. The act of doing so effectively condenses the amount of time you need to reserve for all your important tasks. Time is the only currency to eradicate the debt of insufficient deposits in your account of relationships. Create frequent time to devote without stoppage to the important people in your life. The important members in your life associate the amount of time you spend with them with the amount of love they receive from you. When you spend time with this purpose, do not invite social media or email from work. If the phone rings, do not answer; let it go to voicemail. The person you are sharing this momentous time with will let you know the phone is ringing. Your answer should be, "This is our time, and nothing is more important." Could you imagine how that response will penetrate their hearts. It will make them feel loved, important, worthy.

As you spend meaningful time with the important people in your circumference, you will begin to solidify the connection and appreciation of the individual. When you become too busy to spend quality time with your children you will leave them vulnerable to the opinions and advice of their peers, street lawyers, and other vultures seeking to impose their perception of life.

The third rule is time is imperative for positive outcomes: every goal you want to attain requires time. When you set goals, focus like a laser beam and capture adequate time to achieve the goal. If you are not diligent in securing this time, you will not accomplish the goal.

If you're not gratified with what you're producing in life, consider that time remains constant. If time were an expressway, you would have no control of the pace. You can't stop the flow, and you can't ask it to yield. The only things you can control are the activities you do throughout the day. By rearranging and changing what you do, you can radically alter the productiveness of your time. Devoting two hours a day to the things you value can move you much closer to the destination of your desires. Two hours per day, five days a week, and you can enjoy the weekends off! The more vigorous you become in organizing your deeds, the more sovereignty you will have in your life—literally and figuratively. The best definition for time management is personal management, regulating what you're doing with the precious two hours you dedicate to improving personal development. You will never manage time; therefore, surrender to the ideology that you can only modify your activities.

The more esteemed you feel the more you will devote to managing your time. Respecting what you do and when you do it determines your level of respect to self, and this reciprocates back to you and what you value accordingly. When you resolve the use of your time exceptionally on vicinities of astronomical production, you trigger the law of reversibility as it relates to outcomes. You respect yourself to the scale that you exploit your time. If you use time in a healthy way, it means you respect yourself more.

The principle of time management can effortlessly be ascertained. If you were offered one million dollars to manage time effectively for a whole month, would you be able to do it? You absolutely would manage time to secure the incentive without excuses or barriers. It becomes possible because suddenly the motivation is there. If you elevate your motivation with purpose, you will control the outcomes triumphantly.

When you elect to be a proficient manager of time, there's no need for further instruction. You will just manage your time proficiently. You have, in your power, directives to guide and manage time moving forward when your level of determination is high enough.

If someone had a pistol at the back of your head for a month observing your capacity not to misappropriate time, or else they would shoot you, could you demonstrate excellent time management? You absolutely could! If the motivation is aligned with purpose, you will augment your time well. Managing your time demands you engage in activities that are goal-oriented rather than activities that land on the entertainment axel. Time management requires you to tackle what is vigorous before you take on irrelevant activities. If you're transitioning from incarcerated experiences, you can't be focusing on fun activities. Remember, you should not allow the important things in life to meet at the same road with things that do not matter.

If you embrace working the necessary tasks on the acute hours available to you, at the end of the day, you're ready for rest…but your "rest time" will be made up of low-value activities. If you're habitually working on high-priority outcomes prior to stepping into frivolous, unimportant outcomes, you predictably sculpt the habit of peak performance. The habit of simply targeting things computes positive outcomes. Shallow-thought outcomes become rabbits; they begin multiplying! If you start to focus on inconsequential outcomes, you appoint yourself to work on them without getting anything done. The huge, significant activities become dormant, yet they never evaporate. Then, the critical tasks which can alter your life expendably start to reside in abandonment. Develop the habit of working on goals that are imperative for your growth. More control over your positive outcomes transposes into feeling more positive. The greater enthusiasm you have, the more productive you will feel.

One of the essential steps you must embark on is asserting complete control over the significant matters in your life. Embody control disciplining yourself with urgent matters and you will become legitimately happy.

The motive for time management is imperative. It enables you to control the sequence of events. Time management tools enable you to determine what you will do primarily, what you will do secondarily, and what will not be done whatsoever.

The book *The Three Laws of Performance* by Steve Zaffron and Dave Logan states you're always free to choose what you do or do not do. Your entire life is made up of the results of your choices up to this moment. We always act in perfect harmony with the way we see the world. The way we see the world is a result of our internal dialogue. How we talk to ourselves about the future transforms how we are in the moment.

If you are not happy with your life, it's your responsibility to make pristine choices without delay. Choosing what you're going to do oversees the piloting of your life. You become self-reliant and self-determined. You recognize responsibility all-inclusively rejecting external forces deviating your desired outcomes. Many individuals employed or attending school fulltime have the philosophy of time poverty. Have you felt overwhelmed with an enormous amount of work you need to get done, rationalizing scarcity as the only alternative? We all have sufficient time necessitated to chase our dreams. We all wake up to twenty-four fresh hours every day that we can use to expand our horizons.

As of today, the hours available to you yesterday are annihilated and resting in their proper tomb. It's totally irrelevant how you have consumed time in yesteryear. Whether you're rich or poor, famous, black, white, in prison or in freedom, you get the same number of hours every day.

It's only what you've done or failed to do with those hours that harvest the garden in your life today. Take a moment to reflect and appraise how and with whom you are spending your exquisite hours. Otherwise, they will hold you back. The pursuit of victory is substantial; you don't need to be transporting baggage that doesn't belong to you.

Develop the habit of making decisions in the short-term view, on where you would like to arrive in the long-term outcome. The more you become comprehensive, anticipating outcomes, the more progressive and consequential your thoughts will evolve. The strategic long-term perspective is summarized in delaying gratification. Succeeding is only possible when you self-sacrifice, self-deny, and delay gratification.

Again, the Three Laws of Performance demonstrate how impossible it is to absorb the massive flow of information into our conscious mind. It is rapid-fire data traveling to us in an instant. It defines this inability to receive information to make sound decisions, equipped with the proper facts, activating an intelligent decision that is indiscriminate. The fact that we have made so many bad decisions in the past is based on that description of the facts. We lacked adequate information to make better decisions. The focus I would like to convey, which the authors eloquently articulated, is that it was okay in the past, UP UNTIL NOW!

UP UNTIL NOW, because now we can be cognizant in responding more appropriately to serve our desired outcomes. No more excuses, STARTING NOW. Change the way you think, talk, and follow through on your emotions and actions to bring you what you desire. Become disciplined in procuring short-term pain for long-term gain.

When you're encumbered with vision, values, mission, and goals to organize the activities in your day, you create long-term prospective. You instinctively realign yourself into an optimal trajectory of accumulating positive outcomes. Opulence of long-term perspective spawns short-term acumen, motivating you to allocate time in small amounts.

In amplifying your concentration for productivity, apportion time in ten- to fifteen-minute blocks. It is fundamentally unfeasible to incur negative outcomes or people when you're deliberate in allocating your time in advance, in ten- to fifteen-minute increments. It is your compass to everything you undertake, and with whom. Negative-thinking people assign time in durations of half-days or no time allotment whatsoever. Positive-thinking individuals administer time in terms of minutes The enactment of allotting your time in miniature amounts pledges the use of your time competently. It cultivates positive thoughts and outcomes.

The value of time is defined by how much of your time you are diligently dispensing. Individuals buried in positive thoughts are those exploiting time on trivial outcomes. Remember, time cannot be preserved or substituted. Time is imperative for all and any endeavors in life. Your new best friend in time management should be the word "no." Say it frequently, instilling the word when prompted by anyone or anything bidding for your time on disparate activities. The principle should also be instituted for your money as well. Your money epitomizes the time you have occupied to produce it, so disburse it expediently.

In time management, repetition is the training needed to perfect it. As you embark on the journey of organizing your life and observing your definitive priorities, accept that you will slip occasionally. Be committed to the process and yourself. Stay the course. In time, you will advance the habit of high productivity.

The important word to remember in time management is focus. Your ability to focus with lucidity on the valuable use of your time before anything else is imperative. Your ability to discipline yourself by concentrating on the important task is a quality you will need to solidify.

An irrational use of time is prospering with activities that are unusable and hopeless for the achievement of your goals. Develop the habit of asking these questions: Does this have to be done? If so, does it have to be done by me? If yes, then the next question is, does it have to be done now? Here are three important principles of time management. These principles are extremely important.

The first principle is: every action or inaction determines a choice between what's important and what isn't. Your life is the sum of your choices and the order in which you made the decisions. Everything you do is a choice which is planted on your values and priorities. The activity you partake in at any moment informs you and others of what's important to you at that moment in time.

Once resolute to make a choice, it generates power of its own accord. Positive individuals are those making elite choices. It is at this moment of choice between doing one thing or another where your future is decided. Before deciding to commit to anything, ask yourself: what is important to me in this moment? What is the best value for this time? How does the decision line up with my values?

The second rule is the law of excluded alternatives. This means that doing one thing will result in not doing something else. Because time is limited, whenever you choose to engage in one activity, you are simultaneously choosing not to engage in all other activities that are open to you at that moment. If you go to a concert on Friday night, you cannot go to another at the same time. If you take one full time job, you cannot take another.

If you married one person, you cannot marry someone else. Life is a series of choices among alternatives. Take time to reflect on the ramifications of your choices in advance. It is the price or cost of that decision. An accurate prediction in an assessment of secondary consequence is a key measure of intelligence and competence. Your ability to accurately predict what is likely to happen because of doing or not doing something will save you from a lot of drama.

My training and practice in prison with this principle prepared me extremely well for numerous encounters when I transitioned. I could immediately decipher who and what was an imminent threat to my freedom and recovery, in an instant—by what a person would say or not say, how they act, who's in their circle of friends, how they dressed, their demeanor and attitude about life, the things they consider fun, etc. The information I could gain was endless.

The third time management rule is setting priorities, which also means setting secondary priorities. A priority is something you do repeatedly and quickly. It is of high significance and prominence; it should be residing at the top of your to-do list. Secondary priorities are something you set aside at the beginning. Only after you get your life under control to a certain degree can you start to do things on your agenda that are not important for the pursuit of your goals. Your time is spoken for, just like in an intimate relationship—don't be looking elsewhere.

Here is a great exercise for you. Calculate how many hours you sleep. Then add it to the number of hours you work and/or go to school. The average person will accumulate sixteen hours between both work and sleep.

Now consider how many hours you normally use for hygiene, cooking/eating, traveling to and from work/school, and you should be somewhere near twenty hours. What's left is the available hours for you to work on the things you need to focus to obtain your goals. To have more, you must first do more so you can become more.

If you have reached the twenty hours, that leaves you with four hours. If you watch TV, play video games, go to movies, or do any other frivolous activity that is stealing your limited time, here is the area you need to focus on. There is nothing wrong with entertainment; we all need to find time to escape, but you should always spend more hours in personal growth than you do in entertainment.

Remember Self Inc. You are the one building yourself. You have four hours to change the course of your life; only you can decide how and where to allocate those precious hours.

Therefore, if you are going to do something new you must consciously and deliberately choose to discontinue something old; entering means exiting, taking up, tearing down, starting up, stopping off!

Your ability to set thoughtful secondary priorities will equip you with a key measure of effectiveness to manage time. Could you identify some of the things you're currently engaged in today that are capturing the bulk of your time? Are you watching TV, playing video games, or talking on Facebook or other social media outlets?

What are the things taking up your time? Free up time to pursue the things that are important. Your job is to continually evaluate your activities in advance and determine whether each is really a priority.

Once you determine whether each is a high-value activity, you can then approach it with the tenacity that comes from winning, becoming a true champion. Start on that activity and do it before you do anything else. Use a time planner to keep focused on your goals, activities, and the future direction of your life.

A good planner contains a list where you can record your goals irrespective of when you anticipate its accomplishment. The act of writing down all your activities before you begin will increase your productivity enormously. How do you measure an item on your list? Consider the long-term potential or consequence of doing or not doing that item. Important items are things that have long-term consequences, long-term potential affecting your life. Unimportant items have minor or no consequences at all.

Example: Taking an extra course would upgrade your skills. It would allow you to improve your abilities. That's a phenomenal use of your time. This one occurrence can alter the rest of your life.

On the other hand, a coffee break or going out for lunch or drinks has no potential consequences toward your goals or improving the quality of your life. It is tension relieving, not goal achieving.

A strategy for you to implement is the ABCDE method. To use this method, go over your list of planned activities for the day. Then put a letter next to each activity.

An A activity is something that you must do. Place an A next to every high-value, high-priority task. If you have several A tasks, organize them by priority: A1, A2, A3, etc.

Then put a B next to every activity you should do but which only have mild consequences if they are not done. For example, calling a friend, meeting someone for lunch, or checking something that is on sale is a B activity. If you have more than one B task, organize them as B1, B2, B3, etc.

The rule is to never do a B when you have any A left undone. Only work on your A tasks until they are completed and only then will you turn to your B tasks.

Your C activities are things have no consequences at all. They are nice to do but it does not really matter if you do them or not when you are measuring the value of getting it done. You never do a C task when you have an A or B task left undone.

A D task is something you can delegate. The rule here is to delegate everything you can. This is the only way you can free up time to work on the highest values that shape your optimal results. This is the only way to cultivate a business; you should not be doing it all.

E tasks are prime candidates to eliminate or ignore all together. That goes back to the decision of secondary priorities.

You should eliminate every low-value activity you find to free up more of your time. Only work on the things that are important or make a difference as you embark on the journey of success. This is the very essence of time management, so master it!

Below, please use this template to create your personal planner for setting goals and time management. I found the simplest format to help you grow into it without all the supplementary details an advanced planner has. As you utilize it, remain loyal to reviewing it consistently, and it will begin to speak to you accordingly.

The dialogue derived from the planner is personal to you. The declaration will be instinctive to you only. There are no right or wrong answers. Be open how the thoughts, feelings, and ideas come to you. You will not encounter impediments to augment the principles to your fullest advantage.

PRIORITY	IMPORTANT	THINK ABOUT	FOLLOW UP	DELETE
A	B	C	D	E

1.

2.

3.

4.

5.

6.

7.

8.

	MONDAY	TUESDAY	WEDNESDAY	THURSDAY	FRIDAY	FOLLOW UP	OUTCOMES	NOTES
9:00 a.m.								
9:30 a.m.								
10:00 a.m.								
10:30 a.m.								
11:00 a.m.								
11:30 a.m.								
12:00 p.m.								
12:30 p.m.								
1:00 p.m.								
1:30 p.m.								

	MONDAY	TUESDAY	WEDNESDAY	THURSDAY	FRIDAY	FOLLOW UP	OUTCOMES	NOTES
2:00 p.m								
2:30 p.m.								
3:00 p.m.								
3:30 p.m.								
4:00 p.m.								
4:30 p.m.								
5:00 p.m.								
5:30 p.m.								
6:00 p.m.								

Another important law of time management is the law of force efficiency. This law says that there is never enough time to do everything but there is always enough time to do the most important things.

Here are five questions to ask yourself on a regular basis to make sure you are working on your most important task:

Question #1: What are your highest value activities? What are the things you do that yield the utmost value to your life? Focus all your time and energy on these, on doing them well and doing them promptly.

Question #2: What are your key results areas? What are the things you do where specific outcomes are expected? Focus on these and continue getting better each week, each month, and each year.

Question #3: What have you been hired to accomplish? Why are you paid at work?

Question #4: What can you and only you do, which, if done, will make a drastic improvement in your life? There is only one answer for this question at any given time. This is the one thing you should be working on until its completion. If you're working on two simultaneously, you are out of focus and off track from your definitive purpose. There can only be one at a time. Ideally, you are gainfully employed as you structure that purpose.

Question #5: What is the most valuable use of my time right now? Ask yourself this question every time you find yourself procrastinating or engaged in frivolous activities. Compare your current activities with this question. All planning, goal setting, and time management ultimately grows your ability to develop with precision the answer to this question. Answer this question every single day!

Self-discipline is a quantitative asset of time management. The best definition of self-discipline comes from Elbert Hubbard: self-discipline is the ability to make yourself do what you should do, when you should do it, whether you feel like it or not. Once you have set your clear priorities about the best use of your time, you need the ability to discipline yourself and focus single-mindedly on that one task. Stay with it until it is completely done. "Single-mindedly" is a powerful purview in time management. This means you do one thing, the most urgent thing on your itinerary. Your ability to establish the habit of single-mindedness will increase productivity immensely.

Once you have cherry-picked the most critical assignment, support it with a perseverance. Develop a formidable action-oriented focus. Nothing will move you ahead more than finalizing your most domineering task expeditiously and proficiently. Whenever you feel distracted say to yourself, "Back to work." If you find yourself procrastinating, say to yourself, "Do it now." The more you work on high-priority tasks, the better you will feel when you complete and accomplish the important matters on your agenda. You authenticate an explosion of energy and self-esteem.

Successful people know all the specific details and the explicit order of priority regarding their time. They discipline themselves to persist until they have completed the targeted task. They are promoted faster and paid more. Employees and management get paid differently. From the first day of employment, they do not see themselves as an employee. They feel, act, and walk like a manager, supervisor, or the CEO of Self Inc., creating self-branding and building equity in their stock options. This simple formula is easy to execute if you just trust the process and work it until achieving your life's desires. What is the ultimate definition, according to your values and goals of success, right now, today?

10

PUTTING IT TOGETHER

Here is a checklist to congregate everything we have covered. Feel free to tweak it in a manner conducive to you and what you want to accomplish. You may find yourself going back multiple times to rearrange the order or the process. Be gentle with yourself and allow yourself the time to master these principles. Whatever you do, do not give up. Do not quit, do not get discouraged. Keep gentle reminders to yourself that this will take everything you have, but you're doing it so you can get everything you want. I wish you all the best as you start your climb. It will not be long now!

Question #1: What is the vision for creating the new you, in the ideal situation, if everything was perfect?

Question #2: Where, how, and when do you begin?

Question #3: What are the family, social, and self-values that must be eliminated and restructured?

Question #4: What would your new foundation of values prioritizing the order of importance look like?

For example: my personal values start with God, then Family, then Work, in that order. Nothing comes before God, not even money. Then nothing comes before my family, including money. If what I do after does not infringe with God or my family, I can step into making money, which comes with work, my third value.

Question #5: From this point forward, whatever thoughts you put together should be your dominant thoughts.

Are you identifying these thoughts? This is what you should be thinking about, most of the time!

Question #6: What are the steps you can take to achieve a 0.5 percent growth on a weekly basis?

Question #7: Are you incorporating the beliefs of change into your new regime?

Question #8: Are you implementing the seven orientations of success?

Question #9: Are you cognizant of your old and new self-concepts?

Question #10: Are you accessing both conscious and subconscious disciplines that are congruent with your new aspirations and goals?

Question #11: Are you taking full responsibility for everything that is happening in your life?

Question #12: Are you striving to evolve with integrity and self-discipline, fortifying your character?

Question #13: Are you clear with what you want and what will make you happy?

Question #14: Are you working on your health, relationships, meaningful work, and finances?

Question #15: Have you established goals in your personal, family, financial, career, health, education, social, and spiritual lives?

Question #16: Are you in control of managing your life?

Question #17: What do your time and the activities you are partaking in look like?

Question #18: Are you utilizing the planner for setting goals and scheduling your time in advance?

Question #19: Are you struggling to create an order, a priority, or a discipline in any of the above areas?

Question #20: Do you have the determination to master all the principles?

Question #21: Are you willing to accept, without making excuses, that to have more you must first do more?

Question #22: Do you agree with this statement: "to have something you never had requires you to become someone you never been"?

Question #23: Are you ready to receive and commit to the next chapters in your life as an epic star?

Question #24: Who is the most important person in the world?

Question #25: What is the most important thing you do after reading the book?

These were the twenty-five questions I put together to give you a template. If you diligently put in the effort and commitment, you will unleash the core of greatness within you. If you can answer the questions, articulate them, and explain them to others, your foundation will be solid with these pillars. You will guarantee yourself a seat on the bus of *three* and abolish any possibility of ever going back to prison.

That is the goal of the book. This is our definition of success.

You can go home and find any job whatsoever—if you never go back to prison, you have achieved amazing success. That is the first floor, or your foundation. Then, you can start the process of expanding—and there are so many ways to build a high-riser. Focus on five small business endeavors that generate $100 a week, plus your regular job. If you got paid from work $500 a week, you will now have $1000 in cashflow every week. Money is arriving from multiple sources. Do not concern yourself with how you will make money when you come home; you're going to make money!

Here's another template for you to drive through your formative years. This is the genesis of your values and beliefs. These attributes walked with you, side by side, through all your relationships and issues with money, work, work ethic, and aspirations. What you deem possible for you, the fears that held you back, and the emotional parts of your life have kept you in a mental prison. This is personal to you; there are no right or wrong answers. Just the raw and authentic emotions you've experienced and how they shape your thoughts and outcomes throughout your life, up until now.

We look at our families not to find fault, but to get a realistic picture of what was healthy and unhealthy so we can grow, heal, and mature into our authentic selves.

Fill in the first three questions through the eyes of your childhood (between four and eleven years old).

1. Next to each family member (parents, grandparents, siblings, and children) write down two or three adjectives describing them.

2. On the lines between your parents describe their marriage(s). Describe your grandparents' marriages, and then your own marriage.

3. Use the following terms and definitions to depict the relationship between family members.

    Cut-offs: avoiding communication or contact.

    Conflict: issues don't get resolved.

    Enmeshment: pressure is created for family members to think, feel, and act alike. (e.g. You say "yes" to a family event because you don't want to deal with someone's disapproval).

    Abuse: severe crossing of personal boundaries, whether be sexual, emotional, or physical, severely injuring the dignity and humanity of another.

    Distant/Poor: low or minimal emotional connection between family members.

4. Next to your name, describe your role in the family system (e.g. the scapegoat, the golden child, the victim, the fixer, the hero, the care-taker, the problem solver, the baby, the screw up, the peacemaker).

Lastly, consider how your birth order may have affected your place in the family and the ways you related to your family members.

5. On the right side of your paper, note generational themes (e.g. addictions, affairs, losses, abuse, divorce, depression, mental ill-ness, abortions, children born out of wedlock, etc.).

6. On the left side of your paper, note "earthquake events" in your family history (e.g. deaths, abuse, suicide, war, cancer, business collapse, affairs, immigration from another country, etc.).

7. Summarize here the "life message(s)" you received from your mother/caretaker?

8. Father/caretaker?

9. What are one or two insights you are becoming aware of about how your family (or others) impacted who you are today?

10. Name one or two specific ways this is impacting your ability to receive and give love, or any other attribute that doesn't come easy for you.

How did you internalize the following words? Define them clearly.

Marriage	Sex
Intimacy	Health
Time	Money
Work	Children
Friends	Relatives
Spirituality	Home
Death	Rest

Marriage

What is the purpose of marriage to me?

What does "making marriage first" mean to me?

What do I need to do help marriage grow?

What are the things that may interfere with my marriage?

Is it possible you're not ready for marriage or will choose not to marry at all?

Sex/Intimacy

Is there anything that hinders me from daily affirmation?

Am I aware that sex is a language?

What do I express through physical expression of affections?

Do I communicate my desire to be one with my partner?

Health

What are my goals for maintaining great health or improving my health?

How does the food I eat relate to my desired expectation of health?

What are the hopes and responsibilities I have when someone gets sick?

Time

Do I respect the use of other people's time?

Do I give adequate time to the important people in my life?

Do we make plans for each other's time without consultation?

Do I find the time to work on myself?

Money

What are my values toward money?

What are my thoughts about people who don't make money?

What are my thoughts about people who do make money?

What are my financial responsibilities?

What do my dreams require, in terms of money?

Work

Am I doing the kind of work I love and want to do?

Does the pressure from work enter into my home?

Do I believe work at home should be valued and is as important as work outside the home?

Is work at home shared equally?

Rest

Do I plan and take frequent vacations?

How do I define rest?

How do I enjoy more rest?

Children

How am I creating an emotionally safe environment for my family?

Do I reflect to my children or significant other how delightful they are through affirmation and affection?

Does my home prioritize intimacy with one another?

Do I offer guidance that will allow my children to grow up with the ability to make sound and responsible decisions?

Friends and Relatives

Am I free to express preferences?

Are we able to connect in disagreement without judging or holding grudges?

Do I contribute to family secrets?

How do I handle a situation when someone is attacking or complaining about a person who is not present to defend themselves?

Spirituality

What are my thoughts and feelings toward spirituality?

Can I share my views with others?

Am I in touch with my inner self?

How can I nurture my inner spirit?

Home

Is my home a place of comfort and nurture for every member of my family?

Do we treat each person with respect no matter their age?

Are we able to say, "I'm sorry," when we make a mistake and ask for forgiveness?

Do we have a structure for reconciliation?

Do we encourage sharing?

Death

How is death viewed and expressed?

Do we treat our dying relatives as if death is not going to happen?

How can we prepare for our own death?

What other questions am I holding about this exercise?

What subject caused the most conflict?

EXPLORING YOUR FAMILY'S EMOTIONAL CONNECTION

Most of us lived with our families for the first eighteen years of our lives. Our homes were significant "classrooms" where we learned how to do life in certain ways.

The following exercise can provide insight into what you learned about emotional connection with others. It explores two of the most powerful factors that shape your ability to connect with others.

1. How did you experience *comfort* (if at all) in your family of origin?

2. How did your family tackle the issue of *safety?*

Please fill in the following to the best of your recollection.

Comfort

How were you comforted as a child when you experienced distress (i.e. when you cried, were angry, hurt, experienced sadness, embarrassment, etc.)?

	Mother	Father	Siblings
Through touch and affection			

Through listening to you talk and responding with insightful questions			
Through validating your feelings			
Through addressing and resolving conflict			

SAFETY

	Mother	Father	Siblings
Describe two or three feelings you felt most often in their presence.			

If you could change one thing about this person, what would it be?			
What, if any-thing, made you feel unsafe in your home when you were growing up?			
What did you do to protect yourself?			

Stress Style	Early Message	Feeling	Internalized Response
Appeaser	Don't impose; it's selfish to ask for things	Fear	Hides anger, pleases others to survive
Blamer	Don't be weak or wrong	Fear	Avoids showing pain, hurt, sign of weakness

Computer	Don't be stupid	Fear	Emotions are dangerous; answers are in things
Distracter	"don't be so serious" "who cares"	Fear	Not equipped to deal with reality, will deviate focus to avoid the issue at hand

Transforming the Appeaser: The appeaser needs to speak on their own behalf. Learn to be sensitive, loving, and caring. Have empathy for others, but do so out of pleasure, not fear.

Transforming the Blamer: The blamer needs to acknowledge their fears or anticipation of pain or disappointment about not getting what they want to arrive at what is possible, what can work—without demolishing others.

Transforming the Computer: The super reasonable needs to stop being afraid of and get in touch with their whole range of emotions. They are probably closest to being cognizant of their own anger, which goes with their disapproval of people who do not perform/conform. Learn how to analyze, problem solve, and plan, *while* taking into consideration both your own and others' feelings.

Transforming the Distracter: The distracter needs to get in touch with their own strength and learn whatever skills and information is needed in order to grapple with reality the way it exists, instead of their illusions, or the way they would like it to be. Learn to play and have fun without avoiding reality as a lifestyle.

Equalizer

I will tell you what I think and feel, without blaming or appeasing you. I will not deny my feelings or yours. I will not ignore the problem. I will invite you to do the same.

Be assertive; don't attack. Take in the feelings and be playful, but don't lose reality. Have a sense of self and the necessary boundaries to feel safe. Unresolved issues by others will bring out your fears and emotions of anger and worthlessness.

FOUR ESSENTIAL CRITERIA FOR SPEAKING

1. Be respectful and tactful. Take the feelings of the other person into consideration, including their facial expressions, tone of voice, and body language.

   Disrespectful – That's a ridiculous idea
   Respectful – That's an interesting idea

2. Be honest. Say what you mean and mean what you say. You have permission to feel your feelings, think your thoughts, and say them, too.

   Dishonest – I don't mind if you are late tonight.
   Honest – I'd like to ask you to be home by 6 p.m.

3. Be clear. Ask questions and make statements. Don't beat around the bush, Be specific.

   Unclear – Tomorrow is going to be such a beautiful day
   Clear – I would really like to go hiking tomorrow, but I would like to have your help finding a good route.

How does your family do communication?

REMEMBER – We speak to others the way we were spoken to. Our family is where we may have picked up our sarcasm, condescending or judgmental tone, etc.

Tomorrow does not have to look like today!

Life is like an endless ocean we feel through waves. Some waves lift us up and some crash at our feet, but no matter what happens today, tomorrow we will wake up to catch the next wave.

Discontentment will follow you where you go. You must begin to train your mind, to be thankful and satisfied with who you are, who you are with, and where you are going. Who you are is informing others what you do. What you do in the now, tells others what you will become.

Make a conscious effort to be content regardless of the situation. When somebody does us wrong, human nature wants to hold on to the hurt and anger, to carry around a bitter grudge.

We think, *I am not going to forgive them.* They do not deserve it. But you are not forgiving for their sake; you are forgiving for your sake. Unforgiveness is a toxin that will contaminate your life. You will not find joy or peace in your life. That is the perfect recipe to revert to yesterdays, we need to stay with all the tomorrows. We must stay in tune with the endless possibilities open to us.

When you forgive, you are not excusing their behavior. You are simply getting the poison out of you. You must forgive so that you can be free. It means stepping into your power everyday, making sure that you consciously make the choice to turn any negative thinking into hope, gratitude, and positive thinking.

You let go of the belief that life is a constant struggle, and create a life of prosperity, creativity, and joy. Remember, no one can take away your joy, your dreams, or the new creative person you are building for tomorrow's possibilities. No one can take it; you must give it away.

That means you are in control until you decide to let someone else control the outcomes and response to every event. If you really want to free yourself from the destructive past, if you want to break off the chains of bondage in your life, all you must do is decide to do it. The book gives you some tools for your toolbox.

It starts with you—today, then tomorrow. Today, you get a do-over. It does not matter what happened yesterday, or who did it. It is time to focus only on tomorrow. Once you have a significant internalization of the twenty-five questions, you are ready to create your own personal mission statement.

On the following pages, you will find a template to create your mission statement. Your personal mission statement will keep you on track with your goals, values, and time, and it will not allow you to deviate. Read it every day, memorize it—whenever you have a moment to recite it, do so, and evoke your emotions to it.

Every year for your birthday is the time to reflect for adjustments. It is your performance evaluation. Ask yourself what should be included in your life for the next year, or discarded. You also want to be evaluating your dedication, focus, and authenticity.

Enter five positive characteristics that define you:

For each characteristic, describe an action you can take to express it:

| |
| |
| |

| **Enter three goals for each:** |
| *Personal goals:* |
| 1. |

2.

3.

Professional goals:

1.

2.

3.

Financial goals:
1.
2.
3.

Select your top three characteristics from the five you picked:
1.
2.

3.

Select your number one goal from your personal, professional, and financial picks:

1.

2.

3.

I will reach my goals by [insert a date]: _____.

Your Personal Mission Statement is in the form of a general and basic statement. Over the days, weeks, months, and years to follow, your Mission Statement will become more detailed and personal to you. You can always review and update it. Make every effort possible not to prematurely implement any changes unless it is total necessary to do so. Now, you simply need the Action Plan to make your Mission Statement a reality. What are the steps, and who are the people you need to assist in the flow with the endeavor? What is the order of tasks you need to concentrate on to achieve your goal expeditiously?

11

RULE OF LIFE

What do I think about, most of the time? I think about my dreams and my goals. I deliberately and actively arrange my dreams with my values. Then, I transfer it all to my planner, where the vision is cultivated into my personal mission statement and an action plan to execute it. The hours, days, weeks, and months are forecast to permeate the focus and discipline I will need to arrive at the specific goal. I consecrate my time to allocate the activities for the culmination of what I aspire for. To an extent, it is all I think about and feel like achievement is imminent. I am totally hyperconscious, shaping all the elements coherently. I am imputing by design, in advance, I am evoking the emotions and mindset that will deliver the output in my life as I have commanded. There is a potent tool and ideology I incorporate as a pivotal addition to supplement all the principles here. It is called the Rule of Life, introduced and taught to me by Pastor Pete Scazzero in New York City. We need to inaugurate the rules of life; otherwise, life will rule us. There is nothing in the middle. It must be one or the other. You must take responsibility for the actions of your aspirations and breed the discipline rendering your return.

If you ever danced or played a musical instrument, you understand the importance of rhythm. If you are off beat, it will not feel

CONTEMPLATION:

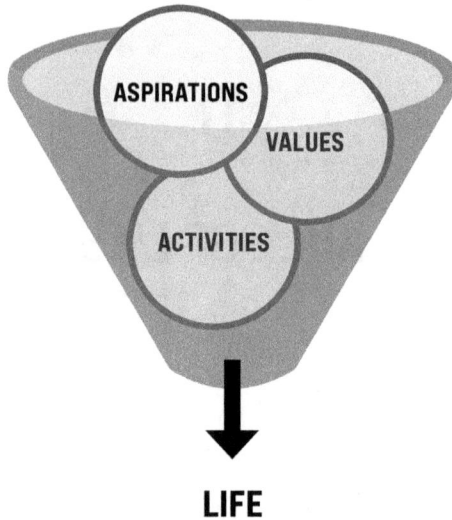

LIFE

right or sound right. Life is lived in the same way. If you are not in tune with the rhythm of life, it will not look right, and it certainly will not feel right. When we are not living right, we are not going to feel right, either. What beat are you dancing to?

CRAFTING A PERSONAL RULE OF LIFE

Step 1: Write down everything you currently do or hope to do that nurtures your spirit and fills you with delight. For example, people, places, activities. List them all.

Step 2: Write down the activities you need to avoid, limit, or eliminate—activities that pull you away from staying anchored to your goals.

Step 3: What are the challenges that will impact your ability to follow through to goal completion and attainment?

Step 4: Take a step back and examine your ROL.

- What is the one thing you must do now?
- What is the cost of pursing the outline on your calendar?
- What do you have to say "no" to?
- Do you have a team to encourage, to give you the support when you need it, and to keep you focused?

Remember, you do not want to be the smartest person in your circle. If you are, you need new friends, a new circle. If you are not extracting any growth or benefits to produce substance in your life, you will go spiritually, emotionally, mentally, and psychologically bankrupt. They will drain you! You need to surround yourself with people who will inspire you. People you can learn from. People you want to emulate. Act like a giraffe, not a turtle. Giraffes stand with their heads fully erected and see way down the field.

Here is a question for you: are you still acting and talking like you're still fourteen, eighteen, or twenty-one years old, or are you aligned with your current age? Will acting your age complement what you want to do, as you step into your fullest potential?

Is there any final adjustment needed to optimize your plan? You should take inventory every ninety days and tweak it where necessary.

Listen to your heart. Women are so blessed with intuition. They have an innate gift to inform themselves of risk, dangers, or pitfalls. The difference between women and men is that, for the most part, women listen to their intuition. Men do not, but it is readily available to us, as well. Take notice when your heart starts to accelerate, when you get sweaty palms, when you begin feeling nervous. Take a moment to ask yourself: where is this coming from?

Close your eyes for a moment and just listen. Something, somehow, has brought you to this point where you are. Every event that has taken place in your life has led you to this moment. The question is, what you will do with this moment? What steps will you take? Will you make the final step? Will you access your greatest gift today? Your intuition, if you develop it, can take you to a new level— a level where your real potential can finally be realized.

The beautiful sounds and music you create will transmit your intuition at just the right frequency with all your mental powers to ascend neurotransmitters in your brain. You start to activate the connection to increase your intuition.

Take baby steps; do not make it impossible. Whatever you decide to do, be sure to keep it simple and realistic. As you create the habits of managing your ROL, your intuition will be authenticated. It is time to finally be real with yourself. When you feel weighed down by anyone or any circumstances, do not give up. You are going to have trouble when you start—embrace the struggles. Once the habit is born, you shift your thinking from hoping to expecting things will come into your life. The paradigm shift is imperative to drive you through the difficult moments. Let us be truly clear—there will be plenty of storms. You are not immune. Buy an umbrella!

You will encounter hundreds of nos. People you love and trust will hurt you. They will lie to you, cheat you, steal from you. You will break up with a partner. Your significant other will cheat on you. People will die and suffer serious illness. You will lose income or jobs. You will not be offered promotions you desere. You may be required to take a demotion. The reality is, something always come up. Something will always show up. It's called life.

You are still accountable to yourself and to others. You are still responsible to yourself and to others. You still must make it happen for youself so you can be able to make it happen for others. You still must live your life, and, in doing so, you will inspire others to live. Here, within, is where life is being lived to the fullest, with purpose, vision, and fruitfulness. The happiest moments in my life come not from money, sex, or drugs, but by being present in these moments.

Living with this type of integrity to myself invigorates my character. The ultimate definition of character is what others will say about you. When you die, how many people will be at your funeral? What will they say? What are the pictures and the jargon they will use to describe your legacy? What is it you do when nobody is looking? What is it you do when it is time for you to do the right thing, to step up?

Here, we end. You are ready to do the right thing. You are ready to step up and live your life as only you can—and to the fullest. I leave you with the pen and the pages you will need to complete your new epic life!

CLOSING REMARKS

On behalf of the entire team at Set Your Thoughts Free, we want to say thank you to all who have contributed to this work over the years—especially the loyal and faithful followers from the WITO Inc. days. I am so humble that you have spent time being with us, reading our (many) emails, hosting countless workshops, and so much more—from the ministry work at the prison ministry to the volunteers, the legal team, and all of those who did the small tasks that led to the big moments in our history—thank you.

This is a time to acknowledge with gratitude this amazing work we are in. We are fortunate to work closely with so many smart friends and partners who are equally as passionate about the work of reentry. When I got home in 2010, the reentry world was loaded with barriers. Today, it has profoundly changed. How we look at opportunities, solve problems, and do the work on the ground has revolutionized since then. Each of you has helped us learn more, research deeper, stretch ourselves, and become better at our jobs and achieving outcomes.

I am excited about the work ahead as we continue to validate new pathways to employment based on skills and competencies.

Companies are beginning to reduce the barriers to entry and shift the way they hire, train, and advance talent. You guys are coming home at the right freaking time, for sure. The work ahead is still a mountain, but we can see the top now. We continue our focus with a demand-driven approach, opening opportunities for others to gain employment and advancement to higher paying jobs.

We at Set Your Thoughts Free feel confident that the future will be more than "all right," as so many smart and passionate people continue to join forces, to build upon, and *imagine* the next stage of eradicating barriers for a successful transition.

The future is guaranteed to *not* be the same as it has been over the last twelve years...because *shift happens!* I want to extend my love and loyalty to all our partners and friends, with special gratitude to the WITO Inc. Board of Directors and the incredible funders who always believed in our work. Thank you for the thousands of dollars in donations and the abundant hours of real work, real pain, and real sacrifice. We like to extend our gratitude to the enormous contributions made toward the furtherance of our work. We aim to build a community of people affected by the social stigma of being in prison.

Our mission is to equip incarcerated individuals with Godly principles, financial empowerment, and transforming values so they unlock the door to success. Our vision is to create a safe place for the reinvigoration of our returning members and to optimize their ability for living productive lives. We want to help them leave a meaningful legacy.

My mission is to share God's grace, power, and glory, with the purpose of sharing hope, breaking bondages, and experiencing the fullness of God's perfect peace.

FROM THE PRISON YARD
To a New World of Awesome Experiences

I want to share the following pictures to give a visual of what life looks like when you're drug- and jail-free. You will have the opportunity to rebuild relationships, build new ones, go to places you never imagined, and celebrate life without any chemicals in your system. People struggling with addiction understand what I'm talking about, here. My main objective in sharing these dear and personal memories I've accrued is to illustrate some possibilities available for you, as well. Sometimes, seeing it in a picture can trigger something inside of us. All you must do is stay drug- and jail-free. Remember, there are no limits to what you can become, what you can do, and where you can go.

"Give a man a fish and you feed him for a day; teach a man to fish and you feed him for a lifetime." There is an enormous ocean open to you through the words and principles in this book. All you must do is catch the freaking fish, cook that sucker, and devour it with all your heart!

bon appétit!
God bless you, my brothers and sisters!

MILESTONES

Released ID

My release from prison

First day home

Ten years celebrating sobriety

Last day of parole

Bus competition Defy

Graduation Defy

Kareem "Biggs" Burke
Co-founder Roc-A-Fella

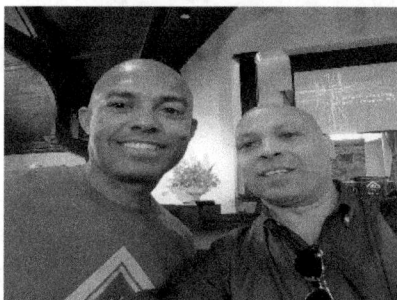

Mariano Rivera
Yankee Legion Hall of Famer

*Playing with jazz musician
Demetrios Kathari*

Christian rap group XOXO

Christian rapper Teddy

Musician Raun Barreto

Workshop Osborne Bronx

Workshop Bronx High School 161st Street

Celebrating re-entry in Harlem

Workshop Jamiaca Queens

Workshop Youth Program Bronx

Workshop CS6 Bronx

Workshop Flushing Queens

Workshop Women's Re-Entry

Workshop Tito Puente School

Workshop Junior High School 127 Bronx

Speaking Upstate NY

Speaking Sobro Bronx

Workshop Bread Of Life BK

Speaking Harlem Vil Academy

Stop Incarceration Forum
Fortune~Castle Harlem

Speaking New Rochelle Ny
Women Breaking the Cycle

Speaking Jersey City

Workshop Rev Q Youth Program

*Speaking at Ban the Box
Suny Board of Directors*

*Workshop at the Mission
Homeless Shelter downtown*

Inaguration party of WITO Inc.

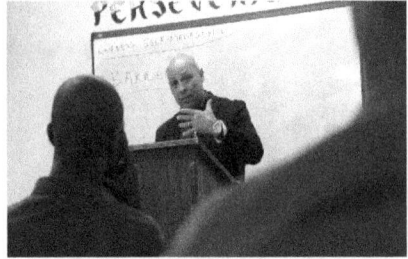

Documentary of WITO Inc.
Edgecomb State Prison, NY
https://youtu.be/EZ27czsAtXM

Personal testimony recording Bayside home
https://youtu.be/a6IqBFfAjAo

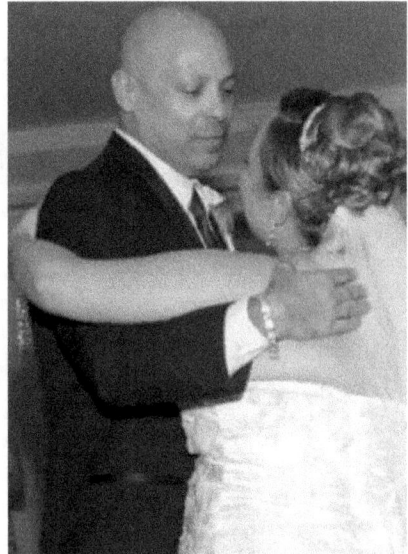

My daughter Brenda

When I received this photo on Father's Day, it validated for me the value of family. What an incredible gift these words gave me. I was blessed to walk and dance with my daughter in her wedding. The joy of receiving this opportunity puts everything into perspective about why I want to stay out of prison and remain drug-free. My kids deserve it, and so do I!

Brenda and Adam   *My oldest granddaughter Brittany*

Adam has brought stability into Brenda's life. He's an awesome provider and has an awesome work ethic. Brittany got free tickets for a Yankees game and invited me. It touched me deeply because she could have taken her boyfriend or any other friend but she chose me. I must be totally honest here, I cried like a baby. What a great feeling, being connected to my emotions in such a real way.

Grandchildren Leanna and Aaliyah

Leanna is the first of my grandchildren going to college with a full scholarship. Aaliyah has music in her blood. She's a phenomenal dancer and likes playing the conga drum just like me.

My daughter Yelitza with Joel and family

Yelitza had a military wedding—that was beautiful to experience. She was the first one I walked down the aisle. Every father dreams of these moments. I got to experience it twice, wow! Joel was a sergeant in the Marine Corp. He has a military pension and is working as a manager for a major retailer. They live in beautiful San Diego, California.

Oldest grandson Elijah   *Granddaughter Jazzy*   *Grandson Justin*

Elijah is currently in ROTC with aspirations to join the Marines after graduating from high school. Jazzy and Justin are both active in baseball, soccer, dancing, and are singers within their church. It's an awesome blessing for me as I witness from afar the lifestyle they're growing up in. The schools are superior compared to anything in the New York City public school system. I miss them like crazy but there's no greater pride and joy knowing they're getting the very best of life in California.

Oldest son Isaiah and family

I value the relationship between Isaiah and me. I have a loving rapport with my son. I love how he seeks my wisdom and experience with important matters in his life. I admired his transparency and being vulnerable with the core issues he deals with. His wife, Dina adheres to family values instilled through her Italian culture. They've been together since their teenage years. Collectively, they have come to the decision nothing is more important than family. They've relocated to Connecticut, just two hours away, which will allow me to see them more frequently.

Granddaughter Jada

Granddaughter Gia

Grandson Xavier

Grandson Roman

Jada, Gia, X

Grandson Roman

When we all lived in the New York, I would get four or five of my grandchildren to celebrate grandchildren day. We did all kinds of fun stuff like going to Giants Stadium with full access to the locker room and the field. We go to the museum, the Bronx Zoo, the movies, or just to spend time together in a park. Elijah, Leanna, Jada, and Gia were the only grandkids I regularly met with. At the time, we all lived in the Bronx so it was a lot easier. These memories are embedded in each one of them forever.

Youngest son Jordan and grandson Noah

Unfortunately, I am not able to speak on Jordan right now. I will say, my heart is broken with the events in his life the last three years. All I can do is continue to pray and hope God reaches his heart through the difficult struggles in his life. I've just started to see my grandson Noah and will do everything within my capabilities to walk with him. I look forward to depositing the values and beliefs of living a meaningful life.

Mom

This is where my heart gets heavy. I've totally forgiven my mom. Yet, I still endure trauma that triggers much pain. I got to a point where it was necessary for me to minimize my communication with her because of the constant bombardment of toxicity. One year on my birthday, she called me not to wish me a happy birthday, but to tell me her brother, one of my attackers, died. I dropped the phone and for a good ten to fifteen minutes was just crying in a fetal position. Here we are, some forty years later, and she still refuses to accept my truth that I was molested by this man. She was still totally oblivious to my feelings and the events that transpired, and that was a lot to absorb. It became totally clear to me, the more I tried to build and grow our relationship, the greater her dysfunction would surface. I can only do biweekly conversations with her; otherwise, it becomes too crazy for me.

My sisters Nancy, Neca, Letty

My sisters Neca, Letty, Nancy

My sister Neca paid for my associate's degree while I was in prison. In addition, she was constantly sending me money for commissary and shipping packages with stuff not ordinarily found in commissary. Letty and Nancy did what they could when they could. They would always visit whenever they came to New York from Florida. During my last visit with them when I traveled to Florida just before the COVID-19 pandemic, my sister Nancy asked why I'm always saying we grew up in a dysfunctional family. I asked her, "Do you think getting sexually molested is normal or functional?" I couldn't believe she was asking me something she clearly knew the answer to. She also experienced sexual abuse. My sister, Nancy, is cut off from me, Neca, and Letty. She brought her son to live with her in my mother's house. My nephew is extremely disrespectful, angry, does drugs, and is constantly talking like he's the only gangster in this world. In addition, they refuse to pay any of the expenses in the house. I was paying the mortgage with Neca and Letty, so I told Nancy she could stay but her son had to go. It did not go well after that. She became angry, talking some crazy stuff and threatening me and my other sisters. To her, we were not problem. I took a few days to process the insanity. I meditated on how to continue with the situation. God's word gave me the answer I needed. I called her and apologized for whatever offended her and told her they could stay but I will no longer pay for any of the bills in the house. We have not spoken since. Preserving your peace can sometimes lead you to separate from difficult people who bring you stress, including some members in your family. You have to live your life without allowing the madness to disturb your peace and the new way of living.

My sisters from Puerto Rico and New Jersey

Sister Vanessa

Sister Ivette

Sister Lourdes

Sister China

My sisters epitomized the true value of family. I was able to feel free, safe, and loved, enjoying each person and each moment. We would all come together without the influence of drugs, alcohol. No guns, no knives, no tearing each other down, cursing, yelling, or fighting. My dysfunctional family taught me to be dysfunctional; I spoke to people the way I was spoken to. My functional family taught me that the love I was given was sufficient to be part of this family. There was nothing wrong with me and I fit in just the way

I am. There was no linkage to conditions being met to receive love. The most important takeaway for me was how every single member of the family made sure to be present at these get-togethers. This revelation spoke of family value in action, how love is received and given in this family.

My Beautiful Wife Odalys

Odalys grew up with my sisters Vanessa and China in Puerto Rico. She's Vanessa's best friend. Odalys was divorced at the time we came in contact with each other. She had removed herself from a twenty-year marriage where she endured all kinds of abuse. There were a lot of scars, minefields, and triggers in her personal abyss. I was so diligent with her, accomodating her fears and struggles with love. I understood her biggest fear was that she would end up in a similar situation of violence and destruction with me.

I was living in New York in 2017; Odalys was here in Rhode Island. I could have pursued any women I wanted—there are plenty of places to go in New York to meet people—but I didn't. We would talk every night until one or two in the morning. We talked so much into the night my daughter Brenda used to joke that we would argue about who should hang up first. She stated she could hear me tell her, "No, you hang up first," and then Odalys would say, "No, you hang up!"

We used to alternate weekends traveling so we could be with each other. Then God closed the gap of distance between us, making a way for me to move in with her in 2018.

The very day I finished packing my stuff to move I received a call in my car from Trans America to tell me the job offer has been recinded due to my background check. I remember it clearly, trying to decide if I should just go back to New York or continue forward to Rhode Island. In a loud voice I yelled to God, "I don't know how you're going to bless me with this, but I'm proclaiming victory over this situation." My intution was so intense it remove the fear and the unknowns, allowing me to fully trust God and move forward in faith. In difficult moments in my life, whenever I surrendered to God, I was always got blessed. I love to tell people that God loves to show off with the way he has blessed me, overly exceeding my own understanding and expections.

When two people come together with a past loaded with abuse, the initial process of living together is intense and difficult. I almost walked away because it was causing me a lot of trauma and anxiety. *My pastor would have none of it.* I remember calling him with a heavy heart telling him I needed to talk.

He came over immediately. That gesture really touched my heart. I have never experienced someone showing up like that to support my fears or pain. Especially from a man. I learned to appreciate and respect him. In doing so, it connected me to God in such a deeper level. God used my pastor to instill the values and principles of marriage from a Christian perspective. It changed the entire direction of our lives and our relationship.

We were attemping to do the impossible. We were looking to built a solid foundation for our relationship based on our own understanding of how to do intimacy, communication, expectation, respect, trust, and understanding boundaries. The reason it was impossible for us is because neither one of us had the proper models for marriage. Based on our experiences of marriage, marriage meant constant arguing, tearing each other down, and living with unresolved conflict. When we agreed to instead let biblical principles be our compass, we eradicated all the barriers to a healthy relationship. Any part of life, when we live it from the lens of solid principles, will result in successful outcomes.

We might have our differences with some things, but they are quickly resolved with the utmost respect for our marriage and maintaining our peace. For example, we sit down to express what we would prefer be said or done. Sitting down facing each other, we express the area of concern. We do it in a loving way, mindful of our body language and the tone we speak in. We have fun doing it and anger or insecurities have no space to occupy because the space is all accounted for with love. You cannot love and hate someone at the same time. It is one or the other—the choice, power, and control is in the way you responsd to any given situation. Every situation you encounter with one another is an opportunity to make a deposit of love or a withdrawal of love.

MY LIFE TODAY

As of April 25, 2023, I will be celebrating seventeen years of sobriety. I will be celebrating thirteen years home from prison as of

August 27th. I am celebrating my third year anniversary to my beautiful wife Odalys. We're currently living in Rhode Island.

We purchased the house we live in during the COVID pandemic peak cycle in real estate, but were so blessed to be buying below market rate. It was an ugly house in the right neighborhood. Here we are, two years later and the combination of upgrades on the entire inside portion of the house plus the current values means we have $73,000 in equity. Equity is the difference between the purchase price and today's worth. Our focus this year is to upgrade the exterior. At the conclusion of the repairs, we're sitting on enormous growth to pursue other goals for ascending our net worth with the focus on retirement within five years. We have other assets which currently has us strategizing an exit to optimize our return and minimize our tax burden. Today, we are actively submerged in our church with Music Ministry and Children Ministry. I am conducting Prison Ministry in Rhode Island and Massachusetts. I am blessed to work with high school seniors teaching financial literacy, entrepreneurship, and life skills workshops in both states as well.

I have an incredible balance spiritually, in my family, and by servicing others. Mentally, I struggle with triggers. Consciously and actively, I resort to my methodical systems of keeping me focused not to get stuck there. My thinking determines what I do, when I am going to do it, and who I'm going to do it with. I must continue to work the principles and strategies for my continued success in every area of my life. I will die with the ideology of setting my thoughts free in ministry, living, and being fully present with the important people in my life, leaving a meaningful legacy for my children and grandchildren. That's my definition of success.

GLORY TO GOD

Who I am and who I am becoming comes from God. He gets all the glory, honor, and praises! I am dedicating the rest of my life to serve God. I was released from prison to set the captives free. The only reason I survived thirty-two gunshots and a life of imprisonment was to answer the calling He has placed in my heart. I will honor the calling with my personal spiritual statement. I am sharing, and will continue to share, God's grace, power, and glory through my testimony with the purpose of depositing hope to break bondages and experience the fullness of God's peace.

GODLY PRINCIPLES

To prosper and be successful in life we need to learn the principles God has set forth in His word and obey them. The Bible tells us if we sow much but bring in little, it may be because we are not living right or in compliance with the principles that God has established for us to abide by (Hag. 1:6-7).

> *Therefore, I urge you, brothers and sisters, in view of God's mercy, to offer your bodies as a living sacrifice, holy and pleasing to God—this is your true and proper worship. Do not conform to the pattern of this world but be transformed by the **renewing of your mind.***
>
> Romans 12:2

The Spirit of the Sovereign Lord is on me, because the Lord has anointed me to proclaim good news to the poor. He has sent me to bind up the brokenhearted, to proclaim freedom for the captives, and release from darkness for the prisoners.

Isaiah 61:1-2

- It is only God's word that allows me to break free from drug addiction without any medication or any program!
- It is only God's word that takes someone who was homeless and turns him into a homeowner multiple times over!
- It is only God's word that took me from raising people's hands in a robbery to raising hands for Jesus.
- It is only God's word that picked me up to overcome low self-esteem, feeling worthless and stupid, to write a book.
- It is only God's word that can take you from a severe state of mental illness and depression to God letting me know, I am lovable, I can experience peace, and I can have a joyful life.
- It is only God's word that takes a man attempting to get killed because he didn't want to go to prison to a man that is dying to go into prisons to minister.

www.ingramcontent.com/pod-product-compliance
Lightning Source LLC
LaVergne TN
LVHW051234080426
835513LV00016B/1585